TO THE RESCUE! COLLECTION

NATIONAL
GEOGRAPHIC

WASHINGTON, D.C.

Inside This BOOK

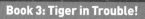

Book 3: Tiger in Trouble!

NITRO: Tiger in Trouble

ETHEREAL: An Albino Bat Baby

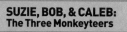

SUZIE, BOB, & CALEB:
The Three Monkeyteers

DON'T MISS:
Animal Friendships!

Book 1

COURAGEOUS CANINE!

And More True Stories of Amazing Animal Heroes

Kelly Milner Halls

Published by the National Geographic Society
John M. Fahey, *Chairman of the Board and Chief Executive Officer*
Declan Moore, *Executive Vice President; President, Publishing and Travel*
Melina Gerosa Bellows, *Executive Vice President; Chief Creative Officer, Books, Kids, and Family*

Prepared by the Book Division
Hector Sierra, *Senior Vice President and General Manager*
Nancy Laties Feresten, *Senior Vice President, Kids Publishing and Media*
Jay Sumner, *Director of Photography, Children's Publishing*
Jennifer Emmett, *Vice President, Editorial Director, Children's Books*
Eva Absher-Schantz, *Design Director, Kids Publishing and Media*
R. Gary Colbert, *Production Director*
Jennifer A. Thornton, *Director of Managing Editorial*

Staff for This Book
Marfé Ferguson Delano, *Project Editor*
Becky Baines, *Editor*
Lisa Jewell, *Illustrations Editor*
David Seager, *Art Director*
Ruthie Thompson, *Designer*
Grace Hill and Michael O'Connor, *Associate Managing Editors*
Joan Gossett, *Production Editor*
Lewis R. Bassford, *Production Manager*
Susan Borke, *Legal and Business Affairs*
Ariane Szu-Tu, *Editorial Assistant*
Callie Broaddus, *Design Production Assistant*
Hillary Moloney, *Illustrations Assistant*

Manufacturing and Quality Management
Phillip L. Schlosser, *Senior Vice President*
Chris Brown, *Vice President, NG Book Manufacturing*
George Bounelis, *Vice President, Production Services*
Nicole Elliott, *Manager*
Rachel Faulise, *Manager*
Robert L. Barr, *Manager*

The National Geographic Society is one of the world's largest nonprofit scientific and educational organizations. Founded in 1888 to "increase and diffuse geographic knowledge," the Society's mission is to inspire people to care about the planet. It reaches more than 400 million people worldwide each month through its official journal, *National Geographic,* and other magazines; National Geographic Channel; television documentaries; music; radio; films; books; DVDs; maps; exhibitions; live events; school publishing programs; interactive media; and merchandise. National Geographic has funded more than 10,000 scientific research, conservation, and exploration projects and supports an education program promoting geographic literacy.

For more information, please visit www.nationalgeographic.com, call 1-800-NGS LINE (647-5463), or write to the following address:
National Geographic Society
1145 17th Street N.W.
Washington, D.C. 20036-4688 U.S.A.

Visit us online at www.nationalgeographic.com/books

For librarians and teachers: www.ngchildrensbooks.org

National Geographic supports K–12 educators with ELA Common Core Resources. Visit natgeoed.org/commoncore for more information.

More for kids from National Geographic: kids.nationalgeographic.com

For information about special discounts for bulk purchases, please contact National Geographic Books Special Sales: ngspecsales@ngs.org

For rights or permissions inquiries, please contact National Geographic Books Subsidiary Rights: ngbookrights@ngs.org

Trade paperback ISBN:
978-1-4263-1396-7
Reinforced library edition ISBN:
978-1-4263-1397-4

Printed in China
14/RRDS/1

Table of CONTENTS

LILLY: COURAGEOUS CANINE

Lilly stands strong on her three legs. Her beautiful golden eyes seem to shine with courage.

Lilly the pit bull is gentle and sweet. She loves to be scratched under her ears.

LOVE at First Sight

For Lilly, it started as an ordinary day. The five-year-old dog paced across her cage at the Animal Rescue League (sounds like LEEG) in Boston, Massachusetts. She ate her breakfast kibble. She curled up on her blanket to take short naps. Once in a while, she even barked with the other dogs. But she mostly seemed sad and lonely. Like the rest of the animals at the shelter, she needed a home.

That March morning in 2009 started out as a regular day for David Lanteigne (sounds like LAN-tane), too. But he was excited. He was going to do something new later that day. Something awesome.

He was going to volunteer at the Animal Rescue League (ARL).

David is a police officer in Boston. He works five days a week helping people. On his day off, he wanted to help homeless dogs. At the shelter, David filled out the forms to become a volunteer. Then he asked if he could meet the canines (sounds like KAY-nines). He meant the dogs. Dogs belong to the group of animals called canines.

"Sure," the ARL workers said. "Come this way."

Slowly, David strolled past the cages. He felt good about the job he had signed up to do. All of the dogs needed loving care, and he was just the guy to deliver it. Then, six cages in, his heart skipped a beat. He was face-to-face with Lilly.

"Hello, sweet girl," he said. Lilly's golden eyes met his. "You have the most beautiful eyes in the world," David told her.

Lilly calmly walked to the edge of her cage where David waited. He gazed into her gentle eyes. Then he noticed deep scars on the dog's left side. There were scars on the top of her head, too. *Lilly has been mistreated,* David thought. *What kind of person could hurt such a warm-hearted dog?*

Lilly pressed her soft brown body against her cage to get closer to David. He felt like she was telling him, *I have been hurt, but I still know how to be good.*

David sat down beside the cage to talk to Lilly. "You *are* a good girl," he whispered. He stroked her fur through the cage. She liked it when he scratched her under her chin and behind her floppy ears. Her personality sparkled like a diamond.

"Can I walk one of the dogs?" David asked an ARL worker. "I think Lilly would like to go outside."

Lilly loved walking with David. They galloped through the grass and down the streets. She gave David dozens of sloppy licks. For man and dog, it was love at first sight. David realized he didn't just want to walk Lilly. He wanted to take her home.

To adopt Lilly, David needed to know if another dog and another person would love her, too. He had to introduce her to his dog, Penny. She's a golden retriever (sounds like ree-TREE-ver). David also wanted Lilly to meet his mom, Christine. David hoped Christine would share Lilly with him. He knew his mom got sad and lonely at times. He hoped taking care of Lilly would make her feel happier.

David drove to his mother's house. She lived about an hour away, in Shirley, Massachusetts. David told her about Lilly.

"Just meet her," he said. "Then you can decide if you like her as much as I do." Christine agreed to go meet Lilly.

Like David, Christine thought Lilly was beautiful. She was a little scared about walking her, though. Lilly is an American pit bull terrier (sounds like TER-ee-er), or pit bull for short. She weighs 70 pounds (32 kg). When she tugged at the leash, Christine could feel how strong she was. But Lilly seemed to understand Christine's fear. She quickly settled down.

Before they took Lilly back inside the shelter, David went to his car. Penny's dog biscuits were in the trunk. He wanted to share them with Lilly. When he popped the trunk open, Lilly jumped inside. She was ready to go home!

What Are Pit Bulls?

The first pit bulls were probably a cross between two kinds of dogs: the English bulldog and the Old English terrier. People in England created the breed about 200 years ago. The dogs were strong, smart, and loyal. They made excellent hunting and watch dogs. In America, farmers used pit bulls to help protect cattle and sheep from wild animals. In the early 1900s, some pit bulls even looked after children. This earned them a special nickname. They were called "nanny dogs."

A few days later, David took Penny to the shelter to meet Lilly. The two dogs got along very well. "That was it," David says. "No matter what, I knew we were adopting Lilly."

David and his mom shared Lilly, but the dog spent most of her time at Christine's house in Shirley. Some people told Christine she should be afraid of keeping a pit bull in her home. They thought all pit bulls were dangerous. They thought the dogs liked to attack people. Christine didn't listen to them. She trusted her son.

David knew the dogs weren't born bad. But some cruel owners force their pit bulls to fight other dogs. These fights are against the law. Sometimes the dogs are badly hurt. Sometimes it's even worse. All of this made David sad.

Being forced to fight can make an animal mean, but kindness can sometimes make it better. Christine believed David when he said Lilly was a loving dog, and he was right. Lilly kept her company when she got lonely. In return, Christine cooked Lilly yummy meals. They went on lots of walks together. Lilly made many new friends as she and Christine walked through town.

Thanks to David and Christine, Lilly had a safe place to live. She had plenty of good food to eat. Best of all, she got lots and lots of love. David and his mom had given her a second chance at life. One day Lilly would return the favor.

Lilly (top) and
Penny (bottom)
both like to hang
out at the park.
They've been
friends ever since
they met.

Chapter 2

LILLY to the RESCUE

Lilly the gentle pit bull and Christine lived a happy life together. David and Penny visited often to play. Sometimes Lilly and Christine went to Boston to see them. The police officer was proud of how his mother cared for Lilly. Then in May 2012, disaster struck.

One night Christine had trouble getting to sleep. So she decided to take Lilly for a late-night stroll. Together, they walked across the railroad tracks near their home.

They had crossed the tracks a thousand times before. But something went wrong that night. Christine suddenly felt dizzy. Lilly stood by her as she wobbled and fell. Then Christine blacked out. She didn't see the bright light shining in the distance, but Lilly did. A freight train was rocketing their way.

The daring dog sprang into action. Lilly barked an urgent warning. Christine did not wake up. Lilly nipped and snapped at her owner's arms and legs. Still nothing, as danger thundered on. Frantic, Lilly began to tug at Christine's clothes. The train drew closer and closer.

Finally, the train engineer saw the dog and woman on the tracks. He tried to stop the heavy train, but it was going too fast. In the nick of time, Lilly dragged Christine off the tracks. Then the dog wrapped her body around the woman. The train hurtled by. The engineer felt a thump.

When the train rolled to a stop, he jumped to the ground. In a panic, he ran back to Lilly and Christine. He knew the train had hit something. "I thought they were dead," he later said. They were not. In fact, Christine didn't have a scratch on her. Lilly was not so lucky.

The engineer called for help. He looked down at the heroic pit bull. Her front right leg was covered in blood. It was badly hurt. She seemed unable to stand. But her golden eyes shined with courage. To his amazement, she was alert and friendly. She was also determined to stay close to Christine.

Police officers, firefighters, and paramedics (sounds like pare-uh-MED-iks) rushed to the scene of the accident. They phoned David. They told him his mother was all right, but Lilly was hurt. David had just started his evening shift in Boston. His boss knew how much he loved Lilly, though. "Go!" he told him. In a flash, David was on his way.

The paramedics wrapped Lilly's injured leg in bandages. They tried to calm her.

Did You Know?

Dogs that are a mix of two pure breeds are called crossbreeds. Dogs that blend several different breeds are called mutts.

Many wounded dogs try to bite people who come near them. Lilly did not. So the paramedics petted and comforted her. They spoke to her softly. "It will be okay, girl," they said. "Help is on the way."

Animal control officers soon arrived to help Lilly. They wrapped her in a blanket and drove her to an emergency clinic for pets. But Lilly's wounds were too serious for the clinic staff to fix. The train had nearly torn her right paw off. It was very, very bad. All the clinic doctors could do was wait for David. They knew he would have some hard choices to make.

When David pulled up to the animal clinic, he was afraid. He knew his mother was safe. *But how badly hurt was Lilly? Would anyone be able to help her? Would she survive?* Tears filled his eyes, just thinking about it. He blinked them away. He needed to focus on helping his dog.

"What should I do?" David asked the clinic doctors. But Lilly was the one that answered. When she heard David's voice, she turned to look at him. She softly wagged her tail. Lilly wasn't giving up. So David wouldn't either.

"I saw the same beautiful eyes I saw when I adopted her," David says. "I felt the same bond."

The clinic doctors suggested David take Lilly to Angell (sounds like ANE-juhl) Animal Medical Center in Boston. They told him it was the best animal hospital in the state. If the doctors there couldn't help Lilly, no one could.

Famous Pit Bulls

FOR THE RED, WHITE & BLUE
TRUE BLUE—
THRU AND THRU
ME & YOU

- In 1904, the Buster Brown company used a pit bull named Tige to sell shoes.

- During World War I (1914–1918), the pit bull was used to represent America on posters and postcards.

- In the 1920s, a series of short movies called "Our Gang" featured a sweet pit bull. It had a black ring around its eye and was named Pansy. Later the movies were renamed "The Little Rascals." Pansy also got a new name—Petey.

Gently, David lifted the dog's broken body. He carried her to his car. He put her on a soft, clean blanket. "Dad's here," he whispered. "Everything is going to be okay."

The 45-minute drive to the animal hospital seemed to take forever. David spoke softly to Lilly most of the way. "Hang on, girl," he told her. "We'll be there soon." When he wasn't talking to Lilly, he fought back tears. He just wanted her to be all right.

Angell doctors were waiting in the emergency room when David carried Lilly in. They scrambled to save her. They quickly eased her pain with medicine and x-rayed her paw. Then they told David that Lilly needed an operation, or surgery (sounds like SIR-juhr-ee). It would be very expensive. David didn't care. "Anything for Lilly," he said. Then he kissed the dog's head.

When the surgery started, David drove home for a shower and a change of clothes. As he toweled off his hair, the phone rang. It was the hospital. Lilly's injuries were far worse than they had first thought. Her hips were broken in several places. Her right leg would have to be removed. The price for the operation soared. It would cost more than ten thousand dollars.

David didn't think twice about the cost. Brave, beautiful Lilly had saved his mother's life. "Do it," he said. "We'll find a way to make it work."

Christine visits Lilly at the animal hospital. On the wall behind them are letters and pictures kids sent to Lilly.

A NEW CAREER

Poor Lilly. She was quite a sight after her surgery. Her body was covered in stitches. Tubes stuck out here and there. "She looked like Frankenstein's monster," David said. The doctors had shaved off Lilly's fur. David could see dozens of bruises on her skin. But she still licked and nuzzled him and her caregivers at the hospital.

Lilly's loving spirit was still strong, even when her body wasn't.

Lilly was tough, too. She hung in there. So did David. But the medical bills were stacking up. He started to worry.

Then came some good luck. The people at the Angell center fell in love with Lilly. They were amazed at how hard she worked to get better. They offered to pay half her medical bills. Word of this began to get around. Newspapers ran stories about the courageous (sounds like cuh-RAY-jus) canine. TV stations sent camera crews. Then kindness spread like wildfire. Lilly's story touched people everywhere. They sent money to help pay her bills. In four days, the center received $76,000!

The Angell center was thrilled. It agreed to cover all of Lilly's medical bills—for life! The rest of the money would go to other animals in need. Lilly's courage had saved David's mother. Now her story would help save other injured animals.

Lilly became a star. Fans sent her dog cookies and stuffed animals. She got "get well" cards and even a fancy "get well" collar. Kids drew pictures and mailed them to her. Dog owners sent her pictures of their own dogs. Soon, hundreds of photos and cards covered Lilly's room at the hospital.

When she was well enough, Lilly started physical therapy (sounds like

FIZ-uh-kul THER-uh-pee). People in physical therapy do special exercises to help them get better. So how did Lilly do physical therapy? On a special doggy treadmill—in the water! First, the therapist put her into a special harness, or set of straps. This kept Lilly afloat, kind of like a life jacket. Then Lilly did a three-legged walk on the treadmill. This helped her build up the muscles (sounds like MUS-uhls) in her legs and hips.

The treadmill worked. Lilly's muscles got stronger. Next, it was time to try swimming. Again, the therapist strapped her into the special harness. Then Lilly paddled around the pool. Little by little, day by day, she grew stronger.

Finally, the doctors decided Lilly was well enough to go home. Hooray! But she still had a lot of healing to do. David and Christine would have to help her a lot. They would have to keep her from trying to walk or run too soon. And they would have to take her to physical therapy every week.

Christine was fine now. But she was heartbroken by what Lilly had been through. She thought it would be best if the dog stayed at David's house. She still saw Lilly almost every day, though. The brave dog had helped her when she needed it most. Now it was Christine's turn. When David went to work, Christine stayed with Lilly. When he worked late at night, she slept by Lilly's side.

Wild Relatives

The dogs we keep as pets or working animals are called domestic dogs. No matter what their size or shape, all domestic dogs are the same species (sounds like SPEE-sheez), or kind, of dog. The other 35 species of the dog family are a wild bunch. Really! They're called wild dogs, and they include wolves, foxes, and coyotes. Jackals and dingoes are also wild dogs. The smallest wild dog is a tiny fox called a fennec (sounds like FIH-nick), shown here. It weighs about 2 to 3 pounds (1 to 1.5 kg).

Together, David and Christine made sure the dog was never alone. With their loving care, Lilly learned to walk again. She only had three legs, but that was enough!

One day David took Lilly to the park. They came across some elderly women who were enjoying the sun. At first, the women were afraid of Lilly. They thought pit bulls were attack dogs. Then they noticed Lilly's missing leg. They began talking with David. He told them Lilly's story. They began petting the gentle dog. They saw how sweet she was.

"Those five ladies changed their minds," David says. That got him thinking. *Lilly made the women in the park rethink their fear of pit bulls. Could she change other minds?* Turns out, the answer was yes.

Today, Lilly still goes to physical therapy once a week. But that's not all. "People want to meet Lilly," David says. The invitations roll in. She gets invited to schools, senior citizen centers, and more. David takes her as often as he can.

"We are changing how people think about pit bulls," David says. "They do have a bad rap right now. But look at Lilly. Even after what she's been through, she is loving and caring. She's a super-friendly dog. She shows the true nature of the pit bull."

Volunteers helped David create a special group to help more dogs. It's called the "Lilly the Hero Pit Bull" Fund. They sell

T-shirts and stickers at Lilly's special events to raise money. That money helps pay for food and shelter for homeless pit bulls. It also helps provide medical care for wounded pit bulls.

David hopes that in the future Lilly can do even more good. Perhaps she can visit injured soldiers or kids who have been badly hurt. David hopes she can help them feel they are not alone in their struggle to get well. If she can live a good life with three legs, maybe they'll feel hopeful, too.

No matter what the future holds, Lilly is happy to be alive. She gobbles her dinner and enjoys a treat now and then. She runs and plays like other dogs, even with one leg missing. Best of all, she has people who love her. Just as she loves them!

Bottlenose dolphins are fast, strong, curious, and clever. Some are also heroic.

DOLPHINS: DARING RESCUERS

Surfer Todd
Endris catches
a ride on an
ocean wave.

SHARK Attack!

Imagine if you could go surfing every day! Todd Endris does. He lives near the beach in Marina (sounds like ma-REE-nuh), California. Todd started surfing when he was 16 years old and fell in love with the sport. He almost never misses a day on the water. But on the morning of August 28, 2007, his surfing days nearly came to an end. So did his life.

It was his father's birthday. Todd was taking the day off from work. He planned to go to his dad's party. But he had a little time before it started. He decided to hit the waves at Marina State Beach.

Todd put on his wet suit. The close-fitting rubber suit would help him stay warm in the chilly ocean waters. Then he drove to the beach. It was about 11:30 when he entered the water and paddled out to play.

Marina State Beach is a special place. It is part of the Monterey (sounds like mon-tuh-RAY) Bay National Marine Sanctuary (sounds like SANK-choo-air-ee). The sanctuary stretches along 276 miles (444 km) of coastline from San Francisco to Big Sur, California.

The sanctuary teems with wildlife. It's home to dolphins and whales and many other marine mammals. There are more seabirds than you can shake a feather at: 94 different kinds! There are clams and crabs, and 345 different kinds of fish. Some of these animals are prey (sounds like PRAY). That means they are hunted and eaten by other animals. The animals that do the hunting and eating are called predators (sounds like PRED-uh-ters).

Todd's favorite stretch of the sanctuary included the area nicknamed the "Red Triangle." It's known as the home base for one of the deadliest predators in the sea— the great white shark. Shark attacks happen, and Todd knew it. He also knew they are very, very rare. Between 1959 and

2007, only 50 people in the whole world had been hurt by great whites. That's about one attack a year. Attacks usually happened between late August and November. That's when great whites get hungry for seals.

"It's always in the back of your mind," Todd admits. "You know they are out there." And it was late August. Todd decided to surf anyway.

The tall, blond man paddled out on his six-foot (1.8 m) surfboard and caught a wave. Playful bottlenose dolphins swam through the ocean waters beside him. *Outstanding,* Todd thought, as he rode a wave to shore. He paddled back out to catch another wave. The dolphins went with him.

Shark Snacks

The great white shark in the movie *Jaws* loved to attack and eat people. In reality, sharks rarely dine on humans. They are curious, however. Shark expert A. Peter Klimley says great whites bite things to figure out what they are. "They take a bite, feel them over," he says.

Most great whites release their human victims after a sample bite. People are too bony for their taste. Great whites prefer seals and sea lions, which have thick layers of fat. People are harder to digest.

Some of Todd's human buddies were also surfing. He decided to stop and watch them for a minute. Todd's legs dangled down on either side of his board. He watched his friend Brian Simpson catch a sweet ride. *Awesome,* Todd thought, then . . .

BAM!

Something huge slammed into Todd at 20 miles an hour (32 km/h). It seemed to come out of nowhere. He screamed. Now his friends turned to watch *him*. But they could hardly believe what they saw. An enormous great white shark had rammed Todd hard. He and his surfboard were launched more than 15 feet (4.6 m) into the air. Then the shark waited for him to land.

Rows and rows of sharp, powerful teeth clamped down on Todd's back the instant he hit the water. His surfboard came between his stomach and the shark's bottom teeth. But the giant fish still had Todd's body in its jaws.

The shark began to shake him. Then Todd started the fight of his life. He balled up his fists. He punched the shark again and again. He hoped to hit its eyes, but he had no way of knowing where his fist was landing. Even when he did land a punch, it didn't slow the shark down much. "It was like fighting a car," Todd says.

Blood started to swirl in the splashing water. Todd knew it was his own, but he felt almost no pain. The shark had chomped through many of the nerves in his back. Todd was afraid, but he couldn't give up. "I didn't want to die," he says.

To Todd's surprise, the shark let go! But it was only for a moment. It charged back at Todd. This time it knocked him off his surfboard. Then it opened wide and tried to swallowed Todd's right leg.

Todd started to kick the shark in the face with his left leg. At last, he broke free of the deadly jaws.

Todd knew he needed to swim for the beach. But how could a wounded man escape a shark the size of an SUV? Todd needed a miracle. And that's what he got.

The dolphins started "going absolutely crazy," Todd says. Dolphins leaped out of the water above his head. They darted beneath his bloody leg. They slapped the surface of the water with their flat tails. They even formed a wall with their bodies between Todd and the shark.

Todd's friend Wes Williams saw the whole thing. "At first, I thought, *What did Todd do to make the dolphins mad?*" Wes says. Then he understood. The dolphins were not angry with Todd. They were mad at the shark. The dolphins didn't want to hurt Todd. They wanted to help him.

"Grab your board, Todd!" yelled another friend, Joe Jansen. Joe paddled close. He knew Todd would need help getting to shore. He helped Todd ease his body onto his broken surfboard. Then a soft wave rose and carried them to the safety of the beach.

Dolphins look like they are smiling, but that's just the shape of their mouth.

A POD OF PROTECTORS

Todd didn't know why the dolphins rescued him from the shark. But one thing is for sure, he's not the only person who owes his life to dolphins. Just ask Rob Howe and his 15-year-old daughter Nicole. Along with two of Nicole's friends, they also escaped disaster, thanks to a pod, or group, of dolphins.

It happened on a beautiful

October day in 2004, at a place called Ocean Beach in New Zealand. Rob and Nicole went there for a swim. Nicole's friends Karina Cooper and Helen Slade joined them. Helen was a bit nervous. She had almost drowned in the bay off Ocean Beach when she was a little girl. She hadn't been back to swim there since. But she was older now. She agreed to give it a try.

Rob, Nicole, and Karina were all trained lifeguards. They were off duty that day. The three of them were also endurance (sounds like in-DUR-ence), or long-distance, swimmers. They also knew special ocean rescue techniques. So Helen was in good hands.

Rob and the three teenagers dove into the crashing waves. They headed for a circle of giant rocks. Inside the circle, the water whirled round and round. The girls loved jumping into the swirling water. It was like being inside a giant washing machine. As she was tossed and turned, Nicole cut her leg on one of the rocks. But she didn't care. To her and her friends, bloody gashes from the whirlpool were like battle scars.

Next, Rob suggested they go on a training swim. It was half a mile (800 m) across the width of the bay. He knew Helen wasn't a great swimmer. But he and the other two girls had their lifeguard floats with them. If Helen got tired, she could safely rest on the floats along the way. So off they went.

Dolphin Chit-Chat

Bottlenose dolphins sure are noisy. They click. They chirp. They growl. And they whistle. But one whistle may be more important than all the others. One whistle may be a dolphin's very own name. According to scientists, the dolphins develop their name whistle as babies. Then they use it to announce themselves to their family members for the rest of their lives. That means dolphins may be able to talk to each other like people do, rather than just making sounds.

Nicole never even thought about the blood on her leg. She should have. Blood attracts sharks. Great whites can smell blood from a distance of up to three miles (4.8 km) away.

Halfway across the bay, the swimmers stopped to let Helen rest. Helen used the float. The others treaded water. Then something odd happened. A dolphin darted past them. It was so close, they could have touched it. The swimmers were startled, but they swam on. Soon another dolphin joined the first one. The two of them swam with the humans for a few feet. Then the dolphins started "behaving really weird," Rob says.

They started swimming in tight circles around Rob and the girls. The girls cried out, "What's going on? What's happening?" But Rob had no answers. He'd been close to bottlenose dolphins before. More than 500 of them lived in the waters off Ocean Beach. They liked to watch and gently play with human beings. But this was different from anything he'd ever seen. Especially now that more dolphins were showing up.

Soon seven huge dolphins formed a ring around the frightened people. They herded them together, like dogs herd sheep. Closer and closer they pushed them, until the people could hardly move. Were the dolphins trying to hurt them? The girls and Rob knew that dolphins rarely harm humans, but they had to wonder.

Thirty minutes passed. The girls were cold and tired. They couldn't tread water much longer. Rob needed answers. So he forced his way out of the dolphin circle. Helen went with him. Rob hoped he could get a better look at what was happening. What he saw took his breath away.

A huge shadow moved beneath the circle he left behind. A great white shark was stalking them!

Now Rob understood. The dolphins were trying to keep them safe. And Rob had just made it twice as hard. The dolphins now had two groups to protect, instead of one.

Meanwhile, a lifeguard named Matt Fleet watched the group of swimmers from a distance. He thought they were playing with the dolphins. He and another lifeguard cruised closer in their motorized rescue boat. Matt, who knew Rob and the others, decided to join the fun. He dove into the water. Almost at once, he saw the huge shadow. He recognized the danger—

a great white shark! But there was no turning back. So he joined Nicole and Karina inside the dolphin circle.

Suddenly, the dolphins got more active. Some still swam in close circles around Matt and the two girls. Some dove under their feet. Some loudly slapped their tails against the top of the water. Rob understood why the dolphins were frantic. So did Matt. But it was too loud to explain to the terrified girls. All that was left to do was wait things out and hope for the best.

Almost as quickly as the commotion started, things began to calm down. The dolphins loosened the circle around Nicole, Karina, and Matt. Most of them eventually swam away. Rob and Helen made their way back to the other swimmers. Luckily for them, the great white shark had swum away. It must have decided not to take on so many large dolphins. It was hungry, but not that hungry!

Matt's co-worker rushed the rescue boat to the swimmers' side. Everyone made it safely to the shore. It had started out as a great day for a swim. Now it still was a great day, thanks to the heroic action of so many brave dolphins.

Todd stands by the patch of sea where dolphins saved him from a shark attack. He still loves to surf.

Chapter 3

Unlike Rob and Nicole and their friends, Todd Endris was not out of danger once the dolphins saved him. He was badly hurt. The shark had stripped back the skin on his back like a banana peel. Blood gushed from the deep bite to his leg.

Todd's friends rushed to his side. They dragged him onto the beach.

His buddy Brian Simpson knew how to help. He tied his surfboard leash above the bite on Todd's leg. That helped to slow the blood loss. He tried to help his hurt friend calm down. Someone called 911.

A helicopter rushed Todd to the hospital. For the next six hours, doctors pieced Todd back together, like a jigsaw puzzle. The shark's teeth had nearly poked a hole in one of his lungs. Todd was lucky to be alive.

Todd stayed in the hospital for six days. He left with 500 stitches and 200 staples holding him together. A 40-inch (1-m) scar ran down his back.

Todd went to physical therapy (sounds like FIZ-uh-kul THER-uh-pee). He did special exercises there to help his body heal. Day by day he grew stronger. At night, however, Todd battled bad dreams. Nightmares of giant sharks woke him from his sleep. But he also dreamed of dolphins. Those were good dreams.

Six weeks after the shark attack, Todd felt well enough to face his fears. He hopped into his truck. He drove to Marina State Beach. He carried his brand-new surfboard to the water. Then he paddled out to the place where he'd met the shark. "I had to get on with it," he says. "I'm a surfer at heart."

Todd caught a perfect wave. He rode it all the way to the beach. Later he walked back to his truck. On the way, he thought

> **Did You Know?**
>
> Scientists say bottlenose dolphins can recognize themselves in a mirror.

about everything that had happened. He thought about how he had fought to recover. He thought about how the shark had just swam away.

In the end, Todd was okay with all that. He had survived. He wasn't angry at the shark. True, it had tried to make a meal of him. But Todd understood the predator was just following its nature. Surfers know some animals in the water can be deadly. He was in the shark's space, Todd says, "not the other way around."

Today life is good for Todd. He runs his own aquarium service company. He got married not too long ago. He still surfs almost every day. And he's helping to create technology to defend surfers against shark attacks.

Click, Click, Click

As a bottlenose dolphin swims, it makes clicking sounds—up to 1,000 of them a second! The clicks travel through the water. When they hit an object like a fish or a rock, the sounds bounce back to the dolphin like an echo. By listening to the echoes, the dolphin can tell the size, shape, and location of the object. This is called echolocation (sounds like ek-oh-loh-CAY-shun). Dolphins use echolocation to find food, avoid enemies, and steer clear of boats.

Todd also speaks out for the brave animals that protected him from the great white shark. He's told his story on TV shows. He's been interviewed by magazines and newspapers. He's talked to dolphin researchers. He supports groups that help protect dolphins. Dolphins are Todd's heroes. He is very grateful to them.

"The dolphins defended me from an animal that was going to kill me," he says. "The shark didn't bite me once. He went for me three times. He wanted to eat me. The dolphins stopped him from doing that."

Why did the dolphins protect Todd and the swimmers in New Zealand? It may have been a friendly habit. Dolphins are very social animals. They live in groups called pods. The mothers nurse and protect their babies, called calves, for up to eight years. In fact, all dolphins in a pod look out for each other.

Dolphins have been known to come to the aid of a sick or hurt dolphin. Like all mammals, dolphins breathe air. They go to the water's surface two or three times a minute to take a breath through the blowhole on top of their head. Often a hurt dolphin has trouble swimming up to breathe. Other dolphins may support it with their flippers and help it to the surface.

Scientist Richard Connor of the University of Massachusetts studies dolphin behavior. He says they have emotions like humans do. When dolphins are happy, he says, they "pet and stroke each other in a very gentle way." He also says, "It's easy to tell when they are upset with each other." Dolphins don't show anger on their faces, like humans do. But they do make sounds that signal they are mad.

Scientists say dolphins also show anger with body language. When bottlenose dolphins swarm together and circle, leap, and slap the water, they are sending a message. They are saying, "We mean business!" They are saying, "Back off!"

Great white sharks are big and tough. They can grow up to 20 feet (4.6 m) long and weigh 5,000 pounds (2,268 kg) or more. Bottlenose dolphins are smaller. They can be 14 feet long (4.2 m) and weigh 1,100 pounds (500 kg). But a great white knows a group of angry dolphins can do serious damage. To protect themselves or their young, a group of dolphins may attack and even kill a shark. So even a great white will usually swim away rather than face a pod of angry dolphins.

In Todd's case, the dolphins may have sensed that the shark was a threat to him. Then they acted to protect him. Scientist Rochelle Constantine of the University of Auckland in New Zealand also studies dolphins. She says, "Dolphins are known for helping helpless things." There's no doubt that Todd Endris was helpless after being attacked by the great white. To Todd, there's no doubt that the heroic dolphins saved his life.

Perched on climbing ropes, gorilla hero Binti Jua looks lost in thought.

BINTI JUA AND JAMBO: GORILLA GOOD GUYS

Binti Jua cradles her adorable baby, Koola.

Chapter 1

BOY MEETS GORILLA

It happened quickly, in less than half an hour. But for the parents of one little boy, those minutes felt like forever.

It was August 16, 1996. The mother and father had taken their son to the Brookfield Zoo near Chicago, Illinois. He was three years old. In the afternoon, the family went to see the gorillas. Seven gorillas were in the exhibit that day.

Binti Jua (sounds like BEN-tee WAH) was one of the females. She had a baby named Koola. Koola was 17 months old.

Have you ever seen a gorilla mother and baby together? They are so much fun to watch. Babies tug and tumble. They climb on their moms like jungle gyms. Then, quick as a wink, they cuddle and smooch. Gorilla mothers hug and kiss their babies. The babies hug right back. When they aren't playing or cuddling, gorilla babies ride on their mom's back.

Koola was so cute, she always drew big crowds. Everyone loved to visit her, especially kids. It was exciting.

That afternoon, the three-year-old boy got a little too excited. At one point, his mother looked away. It was only for a moment, but that was all it took. The small boy in a bright red shirt scrambled over the railing. Then, *THUNK*. He fell 18 feet (5.5 m)—almost two stories—down into the gorilla enclosure (sounds like in-KLOH-zhur). When he hit the concrete floor, he was knocked out. He lay there limp as a rag doll.

People gasped in horror. Everyone watching was afraid. No one knew what would happen next. No one knew just how to help. Someone ran to tell the zookeepers what had happened.

The little boy was in terrible danger. Gorillas may be fun to watch, but they are big and they are strong. They don't like surprises like tumbling little boys. Surprises sometimes make gorillas cranky.

Playtime

A newborn gorilla clings to its mother's chest for the first few months of life. Later, it learns to ride on her back. When gorillas turn three, they're ready for fun! Between the ages of three and six, gorillas act a lot like human children do. They spend most of their time playing. They climb trees and swing from branches. They wrestle and tumble. They chase each other round and round and scream with laughter. Sound like anyone you know?

People screamed in fear when one of the gorillas slowly walked toward the child. It was Binti Jua. Little Koola clung to her back.

A paramedic (sounds like pare-uh-MED-ik) named Bill Lambert was watching the gorillas, too. He was there when the boy fell. He even had his video camera rolling. Bill wanted to help the boy. He'd been trained to help in emergencies. But he couldn't reach the child. So he kept filming. He didn't know what to expect. What he captured was an amazing surprise.

It soon became clear that Binti Jua, called Binti for short, didn't want to hurt the boy. She wanted to help him.

Binti scooped up the child's small, still body in her big, furry arms. She carried him across a stream in the gorilla pen. Then she lifted him over a giant log. Binti headed to the zookeeper door at the back of the pen. When she got there, she cradled the boy in her right arm. Koola peeked at the boy from her spot on her mother's back. It was the tiny gorilla's turn to be curious.

The other gorillas also were curious about the boy. One of them growled at him. But Binti Jua wouldn't let the others get close to the child. She rocked him gently. She waited for help to arrive.

Craig Demitros was one of the gorilla experts at the zoo. He was eating lunch when his walkie-talkie went off. Signal 13—an emergency in the gorilla enclosure!

No one had ever fallen in there before, so Craig was surprised. But he knew what to do. He ordered three zookeepers to drive the gorillas into their rooms behind the pen. The zookeepers sprayed streams of water toward the gorillas. This didn't hurt them, but it did help them know which way to go. It also kept them away from Binti Jua and the boy.

Once the other gorillas left the pen, Binti Jua put the boy down. She was very careful with him. Then she followed the other gorillas into the back rooms. Koola still rode on her back.

Now the paramedics could do their job. They rushed the boy to the hospital.

Start to finish, the rescue took only 19 minutes. How did it go so well? The answer is practice, according to Craig. "Our team has safety walks through the enclosures to prepare for emergencies," he says. They'd practiced just a few days before the boy fell.

Being knocked out, or unconscious (sounds like un-CON-shus), also helped the boy. "Because he wasn't crying or screaming, he didn't seem to pose a threat," Craig says. "He also landed on his bottom, not his head. That may have saved his life."

Besides hurting his head, the little boy also had a broken hand. He spent three days in the hospital. Then the doctors said he was well enough to go home. But his parents never revealed his name. They did not want anyone to know who their son was.

For Binti Jua, it was the opposite. People everywhere learned her name. She became a star! Her heroic deed made headlines around the world. TV and radio programs around the world also featured her story.

The Brookfield Zoo's mailbox soon overflowed with letters about Binti Jua. "Congratulations with all our hearts," one group of kids wrote. Lots of kids wrote wanting to know more about her.

Binti even got fancy gifts. One gift was a sparkly, heart-shaped necklace. "Mother of the Year," it said.

Binti Jua munches on one of her favorite snacks. Do you think she knows she's famous?

BRINGING UP BINTI

Everyone agrees that Binti Jua is a hero. But people still wonder why she did what she did. Why did she help the little boy? Curiosity is one theory (sounds like THEER-ee). Craig at the Brookfield Zoo says, "We think she was closest to where the boy actually fell in." So maybe Binti just wanted to check things out.

Or maybe she wanted to trade the boy—for a snack! Sometimes people drop things into the gorilla cage, like cameras and sunglasses. *Oops!* If the gorillas eat these things, it can make them very sick. So the zookeepers have trained the gorillas to bring things that fall into their cage to the zookeeper's door. As a reward, the apes get a yummy food treat. Maybe that's what Binti was hoping for. Maybe that's why she took the child to the door.

Craig says there could be another reason Binti was so gentle with the boy. It may have to do with the way she grew up.

Binti Jua was born in 1988 at the Columbus Zoo in Ohio. Her mother was a gorilla named Lulu. Her father's name was Sunshine. Binti was named after her father.

In the African language called Swahili (sounds like swah-HEE-lee), Binti Jua means "Daughter of Sunshine."

Lulu couldn't make enough milk to feed Binti. The zookeepers were afraid the baby wouldn't survive. So when Binti was three months old, they sent her to the San Francisco Zoo in California. Now she would be raised by humans.

For the rest of her first year, Binti lived with people, not gorillas. Human caretakers held her. Humans fed her. They played with her. They even slept with her. They were with her 24/7, just like a gorilla mother would be. According to the experts at the San Francisco Zoo, Binti Jua grew up feeling safe with humans. Maybe that's why she wasn't scared of the little boy.

As a baby, Binti even played with a little girl. The girl's name was Jennifer. Her mother worked at the zoo. When the two "kids" met, they reached their hands out to touch each other. It was like they were both human children. It was like they were both gorilla babies, too.

After her first birthday, Binti joined the rest of the gorillas at the San Francisco Zoo. It should have been a good thing. But Binti was sad and lonely. She was younger than the others. She didn't really know how to act around them. She bit a little too hard when she played. And she didn't stop playing when the grown-up gorillas got mad. She just didn't fit in. So the zookeepers decided to find her a new home.

Family Fame

Binti Jua isn't the only famous gorilla in her family. Her Aunt Koko is also a star. Koko lives at the Gorilla Foundation in Woodside, California. Her brother is Binti's father, Sunshine. What makes Koko the gorilla famous? She knows how to communicate using American Sign Language. Scientist Penny Patterson taught her how. Penny showed Koko the video of Binti saving the little boy. Then Penny asked her about Binti. Koko signed "lip"—that's her word for *girl*—and "good." In other words, Koko said Binti was a "good girl"!

When she was three years old, Binti moved to the Brookfield Zoo in Illinois. Everyone hoped it would be a better place for her.

Two other three-year-old gorillas lived at the Brookfield Zoo. The zookeepers hoped they would teach Binti Jua how to behave. It wasn't easy. "It was a school of hard knocks," Craig says. He means that Binti had to learn the hard way. She would scream and run. The other two little gorillas would slap and bite. Scream! Run! Slap! Bite! Binti took her lumps. Finally, she figured out how to act around the others. She learned good gorilla manners. Once she did, Binti was truly at home.

When Binti was six, zookeepers learned that she was expecting her first baby. They were excited. They were also a little worried. Binti had learned how to get along with other gorillas. But would she know how to be a gorilla mom? The zookeepers weren't sure.

Newborn gorillas are helpless and tiny. They weigh only about four pounds (2 kg) at birth. They need a lot of care from their mothers. Gorillas learn how to be mothers from their own mothers. But Binti wasn't raised by her mother, Lulu. She was raised by people. So she had to go to gorilla mommy school.

The zookeepers used a furry stuffed animal to train Binti to be a good mom. They wanted her to learn to carry her baby constantly. So they rewarded her with a treat every time she picked up the toy baby.

If she put it down, no treat. Binti soon learned to hold the stuffed animal all the time. The zookeepers showed her how to cradle it. They even taught her how to feed a baby.

Did You Know?

Gorillas live to be about 35 years old in the wild. In zoos they may live to be more than 50.

Binti gave birth to Koola in February 1995. What kind of mom was she? "She was better than we expected," Craig says. "She was a great mom." The fact that Binti was such a good mother might have led her to protect the human child.

Scientist Penny Patterson is the director of the Gorilla Foundation in Woodside, California. She's also thought about why Binti helped the little boy. Binti might have picked up the boy because it was the motherly thing to do. Female gorillas have been known to show caring and helping behaviors. But Penny says it was Binti's intelligence that told her to bring him to the zookeeper door.

Binti Jua still lives at the Brookfield Zoo. She has never had to rescue another human. But she has had more babies. She's been a super mom to them all. And now Binti's a grandmother! Her daughter Koola has a baby of her own. Koola is a terrific mom, too. But that's not a surprise. She learned from the best—Binti Jua.

Full-grown male gorillas, like this one, are called silverbacks. Jambo was a silverback.

Chapter 3

ANOTHER GREAT APE

Binti Jua amazed people everywhere when she cared for the hurt little boy in 1996. She wasn't the first gorilla to be a worldwide hero, though. She wasn't even the first gorilla to guard a human child. Another gorilla did the same thing ten years earlier. This one wasn't a female. It was a big, bold male gorilla named Jambo (sounds like YAM-bo).

Jambo lived at the Durrell Wildlife Park on Jersey, an island off the coast of England. He was a silverback. That's what full-grown male gorillas are called. They get the name from the silver-colored hair on their lower back.

In the wild, a silverback often acts as the leader of a gorilla group, or troop. He guards the troop. He lets the other gorillas know when it's time to feed or travel or sleep.

Sometimes a silverback shows off by hooting. He stands up and beats his chest. He does this when he feels challenged or threatened. When a gorilla acts like this, it can look scary. But gorillas are usually calm and peaceful—unless something disturbs them, that is. And on August 31, 1986, something very disturbing happened.

That day five-year-old Levan Merrit visited the Durrell Wildlife Park. He went with his parents, Steve and Pauline. His brother, Lloyd, and sister, Stephanie, went, too. The family decided to go see the gorillas. When they got there, however, the kids couldn't see anything. A tall wall surrounded the enclosure. The gorillas were hanging out at the bottom of it. It was hard to see them without leaning over the wall. But the wall was too tall for Levan to lean over.

So Levan's father lifted him on top of the wall for a better look. Then he turned to lift Lloyd up, too. That's when Levan decided to stand up. Bad idea! In an instant, he was falling. Steve heard his son scream, but it was too late to catch him. Levan tumbled into the gorilla pen.

Steve's heart pounded with fear. He looked down and saw his son. Levan lay silent at the bottom of the wall. Steve had to try to save him. He started to climb into the pen with Levan. But people stopped him.

"There was blood all over the place," Steve says, "and I couldn't get to him. I thought he was going to be torn to pieces."

Jambo and the other gorillas were frightened by the tiny stranger in their space. So they scattered. They sounded a warning cry. They hooped and hollered. They screamed. Nandi, a female with gorilla babies of her own, approached the boy. Jambo turned her away. He was probably trying to protect her.

What Jambo did next surprised everyone. Brian LeLion got it all on videotape. Jambo approached the boy slowly. He was trying to figure the boy out. Was Levan a threat to his troop?

The silverback looked the boy over. Then he looked up at the crowd above. It was like Jambo was saying, *What is he doing here?*

Experts say it was a good thing Levan wasn't crying. If so, Jambo might have seen him as a threat. But because Levan was quiet, the silverback stayed close. Other gorillas tried to approach the boy. Jambo waved them off.

Kids Can Help

Binti Jua and Jambo protected human children from harm. You can help protect their relatives living in the wild. Here's how:

- Organize a penny drive. Set up jars or cans at school. Ask people to donate pennies. Send the money to a gorilla rescue group.

- Sponsor a baby gorilla! Families or classrooms can donate money to help care for a baby gorilla at the GRACE Center for Rescued Gorillas (http://gorillafund.org).

- Learn about gorilla protection projects at http://animals.nationalgeographic.com/animals/great-apes/.

- Visit your local zoo. Your admission fee helps gorillas, too.

The human crowd looked on in fear.
Someone suggested throwing stones to keep
the gorillas away from the boy. But a wise
person said no. Throwing rocks might upset
the gorillas. Staying calm was the best
thing the crowd could do for Levan.
Because all the people stayed calm, Jambo
did, too. The silverback started to gently
pat the boy on the back.

Scientist Penny Patterson of the
Gorilla Foundation says Jambo was
protecting Levan. She says it's not unusual
for male gorillas to show this kind of
guarding behavior.

Levan was unconscious for ten minutes.
Jambo guarded him the whole time. Then
all of a sudden the quiet ended. Levan
woke up and started to cry. This alarmed

Jambo. The silverback left the little boy. He ran back to the indoor area at the back of the enclosure. The zookeepers had already gathered most of the other gorillas indoors.

One younger male gorilla refused to go inside. His name was Hobbit. He was curious. He ignored the keepers. He darted down to where Levan was crying. What would Hobbit do next? No one knew. It was time for action.

Firefighters were on the scene by now. They lowered paramedic Brian Fox into the gorilla enclosure. "The boy was bleeding and in pain," Brian said. "It was my job to get in the pen and help Levan out."

The zookeepers joined Brian in the pen. They held large sticks. As Hobbit came close, they stood tall. They waved their sticks in the air. They were not trying to hurt Hobbit. Hobbit probably wasn't trying to hurt them, either. They just wanted to scare him away. They wanted to keep everyone safe, gorillas and humans. It worked.

Brian started to treat the cut on the back of Levan's head. But he was afraid the little boy was very badly hurt. There was no time to waste.

The firefighters tossed Brian a rope. He tied it around his body. Then he scooped up Levan. The firefighters pulled and pulled on the rope. They lifted Brian

> **Did You Know?**
>
> Just like humans, gorillas laugh when they are tickled. They also cry when they are hurt or sad. But gorillas cry with sounds. They do not shed tears.

and Levan out of the pen. Then they rushed Levan to the hospital. Levan was very lucky. He would be fine.

The video of the rescue thrilled viewers around the world. People called Jambo a hero. They called him the Gentle Giant. More people came to the zoo to see Jambo. Scientists wanted to study him.

Jambo showed the world a new, gentle side to the giant apes. Binti Jua did, too. Thanks to these gorilla "good guys," two curious little boys lived to see another day.

THE END

INDEX

MORE INFORMATION

To find more information about the animal species featured in this book, check out these books and websites:

Dolphins, by Melissa Stewart, National Geographic, 2010

Face to Face With Gorillas, by Michael Nichols,
National Geographic, 2009

Saving Audie: A Pit Bull Puppy Gets a Second Chance,
by Dorothy Hinshaw Patent, Walker Children's, 2011

Bad Rap Pit Bull Rescue
www.badrap.org

Dian Fossey Gorilla Fund
http://gorillafund.org

The Gorilla Foundation
http://koko.org/foundation

Lilly the Hero Pit Bull
http://lillytheheropitbull.com

National Geographic, "Animals: Bottlenose Dolphins,"
http://animals.nationalgeographic.com/animals/mammals/
bottlenose-dolphin

This book is dedicated to heroic animals and the people who sometimes rescue them all over the world. May we live up to their examples.
—K.M.H.

CREDITS

Thanks to the National Geographic Channel for the photo of Todd Endris on page 38, as seen in Nat Geo WILD's *Shark Attack Experiment: LIVE!*

Inside This Book title page (in order of books, top to bottom): © David R. Lanteigne; Croisy/Shutterstock; Mike Price/Shutterstock; Jason Nuttle; Croisy/Shutterstock; Title page, © Beth Oram 2012; 4-5, © David R. Lanteigne; 6, © David R. Lanteigne; 13, Courtesy of Animal Farm Foundation; 16 (UP), © David R. Lanteigne; 16 (LO), © David R. Lanteigne; 23, National World War I Museum Archives, Kansas City, Missouri; 26, © David R. Lanteigne; 32, Dbajurin/Dreamstime.com; 36-37, Dray van Beeck/Shutterstock; 38, Courtesy of Todd Endris; 43, Sandra Lucas/Dreamstime.com; 48, Anteromite/Shutterstock; 52, Croisy Shutterstock; 58, George Nikitin, PacificCoastNews/Newscom; 63, Willyam Bradberry/Shutterstock; 68-69, Jim Schulz/Chicago Zoological Society; 70, Jim Schulz/Chicago Zoological Society; 74, Petra Wegner/Alamy; 80, Jim Schulz/Chicago Zoological Society; 85, Ron Cohn/Gorilla Foundation/koko.org; 90, © Brian Le Lion; 96, Mike Price/Shutterstock; 102, © Beth Oram 2012

ACKNOWLEDGMENTS

These stories could not have been told without the help of Lilly's owner, Officer David R. Lanteigne; the gorilla keeper at the Brookfield Zoo, Craig Demitros; and other generous experts.

Book 2

DOG FINDS LOST DOLPHINS!

And More True Stories
of Amazing
Animal Heroes

Elizabeth Carney

Published by the National Geographic Society
John M. Fahey, Jr., *Chairman of the Board and Chief Executive Officer*
Timothy T. Kelly, *President*
Declan Moore, *Executive Vice President; President, Publishing and Digital Media*
Melina Gerosa Bellows, *Executive Vice President; Chief Creative Officer, Books, Kids, and Family*

Prepared by the Book Division
Hector Sierra, *Senior Vice President and General Manager*
Nancy Laties Feresten, *Senior Vice President, Editor in Chief, Children's Books*
Jonathan Halling, *Design Director, Books and Children's Publishing*
Jay Sumner, *Director of Photography, Children's Publishing*
Jennifer Emmett, *Editorial Director, Children's Books*
Eva Absher-Schantz, *Managing Art Director, Children's Books*
Carl Mehler, *Director of Maps*
R. Gary Colbert, *Production Director*
Jennifer A. Thornton, *Director of Managing Editorial*

Staff for This Book
Becky Baines, *Project Editor*
Lisa Jewell, *Illustrations Editor*
Eva Absher, *Art Director*
Ruthie Thompson, *Designer*
Grace Hill, *Associate Managing Editor*
Joan Gossett, *Production Editor*
Lewis R. Bassford, *Production Manager*
Susan Borke, *Legal and Business Affairs*
Kate Olesin, *Assistant Editor*
Kathryn Robbins, *Design Production Assistant*
Hillary Moloney, *Illustrations Assistant*

Manufacturing and Quality Management
Christopher A. Liedel, *Chief Financial Officer*
Phillip L. Schlosser, *Senior Vice President*
Chris Brown, *Vice President*
George Bounelis, *Vice President, Production Services*
Nicole Elliott, *Manager*
Rachel Faulise, *Manager*
Robert L. Barr, *Manager*

For more information, please call 1-800-NGS LINE (647-5463) or write to the following address:
National Geographic Society
1145 17th Street N.W.
Washington, D.C. 20036-4688 U.S.A.

Visit us online at nationalgeographic.com/books

For librarians and teachers: ngchildrensbooks.org

National Geographic supports K–12 educators with ELA Common Core Resources. Visit natgeoed.org/commoncore for more information.

More for kids from National Geographic:
kids.nationalgeographic.com

For information about special discounts for bulk purchases, please contact National Geographic Books Special Sales: ngspecsales@ngs.org

For rights or permissions inquiries, please contact National Geographic Books Subsidiary Rights: ngbookrights@ngs.org

Trade paperback
ISBN: 978-1-4263-1031-7
Reinforced library edition
ISBN: 978-1-4263-1032-4

Table of CONTENTS

CLOUD: DOLPHIN RESCUE DOG

Cloud was the first dog to be trained to rescue dolphins.

Scientists do not always know why dolphins and whales get stranded.

Chapter 1

CALL FOR HELP

When Chris Blankenship got an emergency call to report to the beach, he expected it to be busy. And it was!

About 80 dolphins were wriggling and squeaking in the shallow water. A small army of people worked quickly to help them. Team leaders barked orders. Volunteers put on wet suits for their turn in the water. News reporters were there too. They were looking for a big story.

Chris is a dolphin expert. He has seen dolphins and whales stuck on shore before. This time was different. Usually one or two dolphins get stuck in shallow water. Sometimes they get stuck in the twisty roots of mangrove trees. *But 80 dolphins!* Chris thought. *With so many, how do we know that we've found them all?*

Every time a dolphin or whale gets stranded, it is a race against time. The sooner the dolphins are found, the easier it can be to save them. Chris ran his hands over a dolphin's smooth, rubbery skin. He thought how odd it was that such a good swimmer needed help.

Dolphins are perfect for the underwater world. With their strong bodies and sleek fins, they can swim seven times faster than humans. They can hold their breath for more than 15 minutes and dive 2,000 feet (610 m) underwater.

Dolphins are also very smart. They hunt in groups. They make up games to play. They even name themselves using whistling sounds. Many researchers spend their lives learning how dolphins communicate. In a dolphin's world, every click, whistle, and gesture has a meaning.

Yet sometimes dolphins end up in trouble. They can get stuck on a beach. It's a dangerous situation for them. By the time they are found, most stranded dolphins are sick or have died already.

Why would such smart animals swim so close to a beach? We don't really know. Maybe some stranded dolphins have been sick. Maybe pollution in the water confused them. Maybe they got lost during a storm at sea.

In order to find the answer, scientists study stranded dolphins as they try to help them. They look for clues that will help them keep dolphins safe.

Chris and the animal doctors got to work on the stranded dolphins. The first step: Make sure the dolphin can breathe. Dolphins are mammals, like humans. They have lungs and need to breathe air. They take in air through a blowhole on their back, behind their head.

The stranded dolphins were very tired. They couldn't stay up on their bellies or swim on their own. People took turns holding the animals up so they could breathe. They rested the dolphins on their knees to keep their blowholes above water.

The volunteers also kept the dolphins' skin moist by splashing water on their bodies. A dolphin's exposed skin can dry out quickly in the hot Florida sun.

A team examined each dolphin. They had to find out which dolphins were healthy enough to survive in the wild. The healthiest dolphins were helped back to deeper water right away. Sick dolphins were taken to a special hospital. There they were given medicine and food.

Dolphins and Whales

All dolphins and whales are in the same family—a group of animals called cetaceans (SE-TAY-SHUNS). There are more than 80 different types of cetaceans. The common name for the whole cetacean group is "whales."

BALEEN WHALES

Whales are divided into two groups:

TOOTHED WHALES

Dolphins have teeth, so they are part of the toothed whale group.

	Baleen Whales	Toothed Whales
How They Eat	Baleen (BAY-LEEN) whales have comb-like filters in their mouths. They suck in a ton of water and then strain it through the filters.	Toothed whales have a mouth full of shovel-like teeth so they can chew their prey.
What They Eat	Baleen whales eat tiny creatures called krill and plankton that get trapped in their mouths when all of the water filters out.	Toothed whales eat fish, seals, and squid, and some of the bigger whales might eat another whale.
Who They Are	humpback whales, blue whales, and bowhead whales	dolphins, killer whales, pilot whales

Chris popped a fish stuffed with medicine in a dolphin's mouth.

This one is in rough shape, but it seems like a fighter, he thought. Suddenly, a shout got Chris's attention.

"Chris!" yelled a volunteer. "Quick! Come over here!"

Chris ran down the beach to a spot full of mangrove trees. A small group of dolphins were stuck in the trees' thick roots. They must have been separated from the main group. Now it was too late. They were too sick to save.

Chris sighed. *I wish we had some way of locating dolphins. Then we could get to them sooner.*

After that day, Chris kept thinking about what he had seen. He wondered if there was a better way to find lost dolphins. Then Chris started reading about some dogs that worked nearby. They were trained to search for people who get lost on or near the water. The dogs worked along beaches or from boats in the water. They sniffed the air for the missing person's smell. They could even smell objects that were slightly underwater.

Chris wondered: *If dogs can find humans in the water, can they find dolphins too?*

Chris called Beth Smart, the head of the Dolphin and Marine Medical Research Foundation. Beth listened carefully. She liked the idea. Sure, no one had ever used a dog to find beached dolphins or whales. But that didn't mean it was impossible.

Beth agreed to work with Chris on the project. "Let's look for a dog!" she said.

One of Cloud's trainers, Beth Smart, helps sick dolphins recover so they can return to life in the wild.

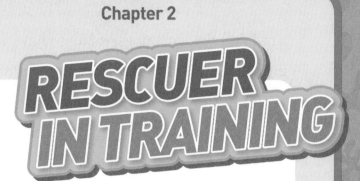

Chapter 2

RESCUER IN TRAINING

There are many different types of dogs. Beth's first job was to figure out what kind of dog they should get.

Beth and Chris needed a dog that was smart. Not every dog could learn to find dolphins. They needed a dog that could swim well. A good swimmer would be safe working in a boat. The dog needed to be friendly and loyal to its handler. Like most dogs, it had to have a great sense of smell. But most important of all, it must love to play. Looking for lost dolphins is like a doggy version of hide-and-seek. The dog would do its best work when it was having fun.

Chris and Beth heard about a smart puppy from a man who trained police dogs. The pup was a Labrador retriever, a kind of dog that is perfect for working around water. They have webbed paws that help them swim. Labs also have an oily coat that keeps them warm and dry. Beth might have found the perfect pup.

But there was one problem. This puppy was a black bundle of fur. Black is the worst color for staying cool in the hot sun. And boy, does it get hot in Florida!

Beth and Chris decided to try her anyway. The puppy, named Cloud, wagged her tail and yipped with delight when she met them. She licked their hands and walked away. She found a nice big tree and curled up beneath it. *Ha!* Chris laughed to himself. *She is already good at finding shade!*

Beth and Chris knew that Cloud needed to be trained to do as she is told before she learned to find dolphins. They called Mike Clark, the owner of a police dog–training facility. Mike had trained lots of dogs, but never one who searched for dolphins. This was going to be fun!

> ## Did You Know?
>
> **Labrador retrievers are named for the place they came from. They helped fishermen on their boats in the Labrador Sea.**

First, Mike had to start with the basics: doggy manners. Cloud learned to sit, stay, and come when called. She practiced walking next to her handler's side while on a leash. She learned to pay attention to Chris and Mike when they gave her commands.

Soon Cloud had learned the basics. She was ready to start learning how to find scents. This type of training makes use of a dog's sniffing superpowers.

A dog's sense of smell works just like a human's. When a dog sniffs the air, tiny bits of odors enter its nose. In the nose, special cells take in the tiny bits. These cells send signals to the brain. Then the brain tells the dog what the smells are.

Dogs have about 220 million of these special cells. That's 40 times more than humans have. Not only that, but the special place in a dog's brain that is used to decode smells is almost twice as large as it is in humans. Scientists think that this means dogs are 1,000 to 10,000 times better at sorting out scents than people are. They get much more information from a whiff of air than people do.

Beth and Chris collected samples of smells from live dolphins. They put the samples on cotton pads. They placed the pads in tubes. Mike let Cloud sniff the tubes. Then he hid the tubes and asked Cloud to find them. Cloud found the tubes by following the trail of their smell. Mike trained her to sit and bark when she found one of the tubes.

"Good girl! That's right, Cloud!" Mike

and Chris praised Cloud for a successful search. Then they gave Cloud one of her favorite treats: lamb and rice doggy biscuits. Cloud gobbled them up.

After a hard day of training, Chris took Cloud for a walk and a game of fetch. At first, Chris tossed tennis balls for Cloud to bring back. Whenever a palm tree was nearby, Cloud trotted back with a coconut instead. Chris laughed. Cloud sure had a knack for finding things!

But Cloud wasn't the only one learning new tricks. Mike taught Chris how to be a good handler for Cloud. A handler's job is to tell the dog what to do and to keep it under control. Chris had to learn hand signals and voice commands. He also keeps the dog safe from danger.

Working Dogs

Dogs make great pets. They are playful, smart, and loving. But many dogs do more than chase balls and snooze under the table. Working dogs do important jobs all over the world.

Avalanche rescue dogs sniff out skiers buried under piles of snow. Police and airports use dogs to sniff for bombs. Other dogs find drugs or rare animals that criminals might be hiding. Guide dogs help people who have trouble seeing get through their busy days.

Finally, Chris had to make sure that Cloud was in the best spot for finding dolphins. It took a lot of practice, but Chris and Cloud were getting better and better every day.

Chris and Cloud went out every day using blood samples from a few kinds of dolphins and whales. They didn't have samples from every kind. But dolphins and whales come from the same family of animals, so Chris felt sure that Cloud could find any type.

After training, Cloud had to pass a test to show she knew how to do her job. She had to show she could follow commands and sniff out smells—on land and in the water. She also had to prove she could behave. Chris was being tested, too. He had to show that he could control Cloud.

The pair passed their final test with ease. Cloud could find the tiniest drop of hidden dolphin scent. Now Chris and Cloud were an official K-9 unit. They could start working. K-9 is the name given to a team made up of a person and a dog. "K-9" sounds like the word "canine," which means dog.

To celebrate, Chris got Cloud a bright orange life vest. It said, "Working Dog. DO NOT PET." Chris didn't want people to mess up her search by distracting her while she was on the job. Chris put the vest on Cloud. She stood proudly and wagged her tail. Now, Cloud was ready to use her remarkable nose to search for dolphins in trouble.

Cloud greets these two dolphins like they are old friends.

Chapter 3

One day Chris gets a call about a possible dolphin stranding. He wakes Cloud from her spot on the porch. He pulls out her orange life vest. Cloud can barely contain herself. She lets out a bark of excitement. Her tail wags wildly. It's like she's saying, "Hurry up! Let's find some dolphins!"

Chris stops to check that they have all their safety gear. They carry life vests, just in case. They have a device that helps them tell where they are and where they are going.

Cloud and Chris can only search for dolphins in waters deep enough for boats. This rule is for Cloud's safety. If the water is too shallow, a boat might get stuck. And finding dolphins by swimming around or running along the beach would be too tiring for Cloud. Also, stranded dolphins are often sick. Cloud could get sick too if she comes too close to one.

Cloud and Chris head for the dock. It's nearly sunset. Soon the moon and the stars will be the only lights in the sky. *This is why we need Cloud,* Chris thinks. *It would be way too hard to see dolphins in the dark.*

Cloud takes her position in the front of the boat. It's 16 feet (4.9 m) long and sits low in the water so Cloud has a good sniffing spot. The boat is named *Cloud's Waterwings*. Cloud stands and sniffs the air. Her nose wriggles constantly. The salty wind ruffles her black coat.

Chris steers the boat toward the spot where someone had reported seeing a beached dolphin. He knows there might not really be a dolphin there. Reports like these are often mistakes. Sometimes what people think is a dolphin is really a pile of garbage or a clump of seaweed. Still, every call must be checked out.

Chris puts Cloud on alert. That means he tells Cloud to sniff just for dolphins and whales. She knows to signal if she smells one. At first, Cloud stands silently. Chris wonders if the report was a mistake.

Suddenly, Cloud starts to bark. She sits, just as she was trained to do. This is Cloud's signal. She smells a dolphin.

Then Chris sees it! A dolphin lies on the beach ahead. Chris calls for help. When a stranded dolphin is found, experts always come to the rescue. They can take the dolphin to the special hospital if it is sick. They can get it out to sea if it is well. If there are a lot of stranded dolphins, they can gather volunteers to watch over the dolphins until they can sort things out.

There's a chance the dolphin has already died. Even so, it is good that Cloud found it. Scientists can study the body. They can see if the dolphin had any diseases. They can find out what it ate, how long it lived, and how many calves, or babies, it had. They can also tell if pollution hurt the dolphin or if it had ever been hit by a ship or caught in fishing gear.

By learning information about a dolphin that didn't survive being stranded, experts might be able to prevent strandings from happening again. If they can figure out the problem, they can try to fix it.

> **Did You Know?**
>
> Dolphins don't drink water. They get all the water they need from the fish they eat.

Chris steers the boat closer to get a better look at the dolphin on the beach. It's alive, but shark bites cover its body. It needs help fast! Even though the dolphin's condition isn't good, Chris praises Cloud. He gives her a treat. She did her job perfectly. Soon the team of experts arrives. They take care of the injured dolphin. Cloud and Chris hurry back to the dock.

Cloud has found six dolphins and whales in trouble. She once even smelled a stranded pilot whale from half a mile away!

Since Cloud has been such a success, Chris and Beth are planning to put more dogs through the training program. Two German shepherds will follow in Cloud's paw prints. Beth plans to provide dogs to people who look for stranded dolphins and whales in other places, too. Many organizations have shown an interest in having a dolphin-finding dog of their own.

Beth is also thinking about other animals that dogs could help rescue.

Whale of a Job

Cloud might be the world's first dolphin search and rescue dog. But she's not the only pup to lend whales a helping paw.

Scientists at the New England Aquarium have been studying right whales. The easiest way to study them is to collect the whales' scat, or poop. The stinky stuff floats on the top of the water for about an hour before sinking. That's where Fargo and Bob come in. These dogs are trained to ride in research boats. They bark when they smell whale poop. Thanks to these dogs, scientists are learning more every day!

Manatees and sea turtles can get stuck on beaches too. Could dogs be trained to help those animals? Beth thinks so. But it would be too confusing for one dog to learn multiple animal smells. So for now, Beth and Chris are working just on dolphin and whale rescue.

Chris hopes that his new dogs will be natural friends to dolphins like Cloud is. He remembers the day of Cloud's final lesson. Chris took Cloud to a marine park so she could learn the difference between sick and healthy dolphins.

"Where are the dolphins, Cloud?" asked Chris.

Cloud ran to the dock and sat down. Two dolphins popped up from the water. Cloud, with her pink tongue dangling, leaned in for a kiss. It was almost like the dolphins knew that Cloud was their friend.

The dolphins followed Cloud's every move. As Cloud walked up the dock, they swam along beside her in the water. When she turned back, they were still right beside her. And Cloud seemed as interested in the dolphins as they were in her. She stayed and watched them play for hours.

Chris grinned. "If I were to leave you alone, you might move right in with them!" he teased. One thing is certain: Man's best friend has room in her heart for dolphins too.

Kasey helps Ned unscrew the cap from a water bottle. They make a great team.

KASEY: MONKEY MIRACLE WORKER

Ned's life changed forever when he injured his spinal cord in a car accident.

Chapter 1

A LIFE CHANGED

The day that changed Ned Sullivan's life started like any other. Ned was a college student in Arizona. He worked at a big sports magazine. It was the perfect job for a sports fan. Ned got good grades and was looking forward to one day working in sports full-time. Then, in the blink of an eye, his world changed. Ned was in a car accident.

An ambulance came and rushed Ned to the hospital. Doctors saw that his brain and spine were badly hurt. They were very worried.

Doctors called Ned's family, who lived across the country. His mom, Ellen, came right away. She wanted to help him get better. Ned needed to be around family. The doctors said the best hope was for Ellen and Ned to fly back across the country to Boston, Massachusetts, where his family lived.

Ellen and Ned made the trip on a special plane that has equipment for medical emergencies. The flight went well. Ned was home where he needed to be, but he was still in bad shape.

Ned needed the help of a machine just

to breathe. He couldn't move, talk, eat, or drink. The only way Ned could communicate was by blinking his eyes.

The doctors got Ned a spelling board. The board lists the letters of the alphabet. Ellen would touch the letters. When she touched the letter Ned wanted, he would blink. Then they would find the next letter in the same way. Slowly, the words built a sentence.

Ned could tell people what he needed using the letter board, but it took a long time. He asked his mom for more help.

Ned worked hard to get better. But his doctors still worried that he might never speak or breathe on his own again. They told this to Ned and his family. Then one day something amazing happened. Ned started breathing on his own.

It's a miracle! Ellen thought. *If he can learn to breathe again, might he be able to do other things some day?*

The doctors were also excited to see what else Ned could do. Ned's family took him to a special hospital. Many experts on these types of injuries worked there. Plus, the hospital had all the right equipment to help Ned with his treatment.

At the new hospital, Ned had to work harder than he ever had. Ned tried to learn how to speak again. He practiced trying to move his arms and legs. He learned how to control a special wheelchair by sipping and puffing into a straw.

Ned had to relearn how to do things that most people don't think about when they do them, like getting out of bed, dressing, bathing, and eating. He had to do them without using his arms or legs. Ned's progress was slow and difficult. But sometimes, a breakthrough would happen.

"Hi, Mom," Ned cheerfully said one day after months of silence. Ned's voice didn't sound the same. His words came out slowly. Ned didn't like that, but his Mom didn't care. She cheered with joy. *Ned could talk again!* Soon after that, Ned could swallow soft foods. Then he could move his hand a little bit. Ned was finally starting to get better.

After almost a year in hospitals, Ned's doctors said he was ready to go home. This made Ned's mom very nervous.

What if he needs me but I'm not in the

room? she thought. *How will I be able to care for him?*

Ned's doctors had an idea. They suggested he get a helper at home.

What can a helper do for me that my mom can't? Ned thought. But the doctors weren't talking about another person. They were talking about a dog!

There are places that carefully train dogs to do things for people who need help. The dogs can open doors and fetch things for them. This might be just the answer for Ned! But Ned didn't like this idea. He told his Mom he didn't want another dog. His family already had two goofy mutts at home.

"We have dogs," Ned said.

Ned's mom accepted his answer.

Staying Safe

Things like biking, diving, and playing on a playground can be great exercise and lots of fun. That's important for your health. But it's also important to remember to use the right safety gear and follow the rules. Most spinal cord injuries occur in people between the ages of 16 and 26. Risky things like running around the pool, diving into shallow water, and biking without a helmet are often to blame. You can lower your risk by knowing what to do. Follow playground and pool rules. Always wear a helmet when you bike or skateboard.

But she still worried about him. She thought that Ned might need some cheering up. He had made great progress in getting better. Still, all of his hard work did not seem to make him much happier. Then Ellen had an idea.

"Hey, Ned, didn't we once see something on the news about trained monkeys?"

Ned shot her a look.

"I'm serious. Remember? Maybe we could look into that."

Ned wasn't buying it.

The very next day, Ned's sisters, Maddie and Anna, went to an assembly at their school. The topic was safety. The students learned about safe habits, like wearing helmets and seat belts. There was a special guest: a working monkey named Ayla. She was trained to help people who couldn't do things for themselves.

Maddie and Anna rushed home to tell their mom and Ned about Ayla. Ellen couldn't believe it. She had seen something about monkey helpers. Could this be the answer they were looking for?

Ned didn't want to get his hopes too high.

"Maybe," he said.

Did You Know?

The first trained helper monkey went to work in 1979.

Kasey when she was just a baby. She had to wait 15 years until she could attend monkey college.

Chapter 2

MONKEY COLLEGE

School was easy for Kasey. She sped through her lessons with ease. Plus she was friendly with all the other students and with the teachers, too. But Kasey wasn't a regular school kid. She was a monkey. And her school was called Monkey College.

Monkey College trains capuchin (sounds like KAH-POO-CHIN) monkeys to help people. It is run by a group called Helping Hands. The capuchin monkeys have perfect fingers and toes for using tools and holding things. They can unscrew the cap of a water bottle, put a disc in a DVD player, and flip a light switch.

Kasey had gone to school for three years. She could pick up and return dropped objects. She could turn the pages of a book. She could even scratch an itch. She was the perfect helper for someone who couldn't use his or her arms and legs. Someone like Ned.

Just like a child, Kasey started learning even before she started school. When she was young, she lived with a human family. There, Kasey got used to the noises and activities that are a part of living with people. This is a very important step in becoming a service monkey.

Around age 15, Kasey was ready to go to college. Like human students, Monkey College students must pass from one grade to the next. Each grade is a little bit harder than the one before.

Kasey's first classroom was a plain room called the Cubicle. Here Kasey learned to copy her teacher. "Monkey see, monkey do" was the name of the game. Kasey earned a tasty treat every time she did exactly what the teacher did.

Megan Talbert was one of Kasey's teachers. She used a baby toy for one of Kasey's lessons. Talbert put plastic rings on a small post. They looked like colored doughnuts. Kasey watched what Megan did. Now, it was her turn. Kasey slid the rings down the post just like her teacher. Megan gave Kasey a spoon of peanut butter. It's one of her favorite foods and served as a reward. "Nice work, Kasey!"

After about a year, Kasey moved to the B Room. Megan went with her. Here, Megan sat in a wheelchair to get Kasey used to it. She did jobs, like pouring a glass of juice, step by step. Kasey learned each step. Then she learned to put all the steps together. Megan also taught Kasey to follow a light pointer. Someone who couldn't point with her fingers could point at something by holding the pointer in her mouth. Then Kasey could get the object the light pointed to and bring it back to the person.

After a year of lessons in the B Room, Kasey was ready for the highest level. It's called the Apartment. This classroom looks like a home. It's an important step in monkey training because it's like the homes where the monkeys will be sent to work.

Kasey and her classmates loved it. They wanted to open all the doors. They wanted to climb all the shelves. They wanted to search through drawers.

Did You Know?

Capuchins are one of the smartest monkeys. They have the ability to use tools and learn new skills more quickly than most other monkeys.

All of the monkeys were allowed time to play and explore. But they had to learn what was a toy and what was not. They had to learn when it was time to work and when it was time to play. They also had to be potty trained.

In the Apartment, Kasey learned to help people by being their arms and legs. She learned how to wash a person's face and scratch itches. She pushed up eyeglasses when they slipped down Megan's nose. She put Megan's hand on the wheelchair's armrest when it fell off. Now, Kasey was a true helper monkey. She was done with school, but there was one important thing left: Kasey needed a person to help.

Megan got a letter from Ellen. She asked Helping Hands for a helper monkey for Ned. The letter said that Ned was part of a big family in a busy home. There were two young girls and two dogs that barked a lot. Older, college-age children were always coming and going. All those things could scare a monkey.

There were good things too. Ned was a young man. He could make friends with a monkey and stay friends for life. Ellen would be home all day. She could help take care of a monkey. The most important thing was that Ned was a hard worker. He put a lot of effort into learning to talk better. Learning to move his arms and legs was difficult, but he tried hard. He never missed a doctor's appointment. Ned was a person who would be very thankful for a monkey's help.

Megan decided Ned should have a monkey. Then she had to choose which monkey would be best for Ned. Like people, monkeys have different personalities. Some monkeys are quiet and calm. Some monkeys are shy. Kasey was bossy, but she was also very friendly and outgoing. Kasey would like Ned and Ellen's busy home.

Megan took Kasey to Ned's home. Then she spent a week teaching the family how to care for Kasey. Megan helped them set up Kasey's cage in Ned's room. She gave them all of Kasey's toys. Kasey's favorite was a black coin purse that zipped open and shut. Megan showed Ellen how to make Kasey's meals: monkey chow, seven times a day.

Finally, it was time for Kasey and Ned to begin working together. Everyone was excited. It was time for Ned to see what Kasey could do.

Calling All Capuchins

Monkey College teaches only capuchin monkeys. Capuchins are very smart. They weigh just six to nine pounds (3 to 4 kg). They are so small they can hitch a ride on a wheelchair.

Capuchins are part of the family of animals called primates. This family includes apes, humans, and all monkeys. Capuchins come from South America. They live for about 40 years. That's four times as long as a dog. A helper monkey can stay with someone much longer than a dog can.

Kasey has helped Ned recover far beyond what anyone imagined.

Chapter 3

MIRACLE MONKEY

"Kasey, come. Sit," Ned asked. Kasey gave Ned a bored look. She hopped up on the coffee table to flip through a magazine instead.

Ned felt sad. *Why doesn't she like me,* he thought.

Before Kasey arrived, Ned and his family couldn't wait to meet her. They thought it would be like getting a new puppy. They thought

Kasey would jump into their arms. They thought she'd hug them and kiss them, and they would all love each other right away.

But the family was forgetting one important thing. Monkeys aren't like dogs. They're more like people. Imagine walking into a house full of strangers. You wouldn't be everyone's friend right away. You would take your time getting to know everyone.

Monkeys are the same way. They watch people. They study how people act. Kasey needed time to get used to her new home. Megan had seen this happen many times. She asked Ned to be patient.

"She'll come around, Ned. Let's try it again, with peanut butter this time."

Megan attached a holder for peanut butter to Ned's wheelchair. Ned could bend his finger just a little. That way he could scoop the peanut butter and give it to Kasey.

With a peanut butter prize, Kasey obeyed. She leaped into Ned's lap and licked her sticky reward. But seconds later, she was back on Megan's shoulder.

"It will take time to make friends with Kasey," Megan told him again.

Kasey wasn't always doing what Ned told her to do. But Ned still couldn't take his eyes off her. She played with her toys. She flipped through a book. She zipped and unzipped her purse. At meals, she twirled with excitement, her black fur puffing up.

Having a monkey is a lot of work.

Feeding, washing, and cleaning up after Kasey was hard for Ned's mom. *This is like having a three-year-old with five arms!* Ellen thought.

Slowly Kasey started to feel at home. She helped Ned more and more. She would get Ned a bottle of water, put a straw in it, and hold it to his mouth. She fetched things quickly. She stayed on his lap after gobbling her peanut butter.

One day, Ned's arm slipped off the wheelchair armrest. Kasey hurried over to put it back without being asked. Another day, Kasey dragged a notepad and pencil onto Ned's lap. She loved to doodle. When she was finished drawing, she put the pencil in Ned's hand. It was like she was saying, *Now it's your turn.*

Soon Kasey was watching Ned just as closely as he was watching her. Kasey learned how much Ned could move. When Ned asked her to get the television remote, she brought it back and held it slightly out of Ned's reach. After Ned stretched for it, Kasey put the remote in his hand. She wrapped his fingers around it, just like she was trained to do.

Kasey repeated these steps with any object Ned asked her to get. In time, Kasey started bringing things to Ned's weaker right hand. She would tap them on his leg, make Ned reach, and then give him the object. Ellen couldn't believe her eyes. This little monkey was making Ned work a little harder every day. She was helping Ned get stronger.

Ellen called Megan to tell her what was happening. She asked if Megan had trained Kasey to do it.

"No, this wasn't part of Kasey's training. She's doing it on her own. But I'm not surprised."

"How can you not be surprised?" asked Ellen. "This is amazing!"

"Kasey is smart. She knows Ned and what he needs to get better."

Over and over, Kasey proved that she knew just what Ned needed. When Ned's body hurt, she crawled onto his chest. She wrapped her tail around his neck. She made deep cooing sounds. Her care made Ned feel better.

One day, Ned's hand slipped and hit the wheelchair controls. They got stuck on "go." The wheelchair crashed into a bed. It started racing toward a window. Kasey started screaming with all her might. She didn't stop until someone ran upstairs and stopped the runaway chair.

As Kasey and Ned's friendship grew, Ned's doctors saw changes in Ned. He had always worked hard to get stronger. But now he was healing faster.

"I think we can thank Kasey for how much better you are moving your arms," said one of Ned's therapists.

Kasey's ways of getting Ned to work harder were working. Ellen sensed that something else was happening, too. Ned wanted to take care of Kasey in return for all she did for him. He wanted to feed her, pet her, and hold her. For the first time since the accident, there was something Ned felt strongly about. He was responsible for Kasey.

When Kasey first came, Ned could hardly move from the neck down. He could barely move his hands. After five years with Kasey, Ned can move his hands, his arms, and his upper body. Ned can now hold Kasey. He can feed her walnuts. He can rub noses with her.

With Kasey at his side, Ned wants to tell the world his story. He and Kasey visit schools and hospitals. They tell kids to stay safe. They also tell them that no problem is too big. With help, you can be strong enough to get through anything.

"Kasey keeps me going. I will keep getting better. Kasey will take me further."

Don't Call Me a Pet

Kasey has made a big difference in Ned's life. When a monkey goes to Monkey College, it can be a big help to a person. But monkeys that haven't been to college are not good pets for humans. Monkeys are not like cats and dogs. They are wild animals, and wild animals can be dangerous. Visit your local zoo or wildlife center to learn more about monkeys.

RATS:
HEROES IN SMALL PACKAGES

This hero rat is doing a training exercise to find land mines.

African giant pouched rats have an incredible sense of smell that scientists are putting to good use.

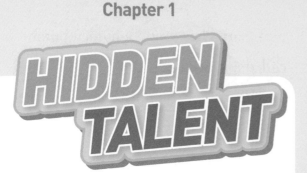

Chapter 1

HIDDEN TALENT

Samo races through the tall grass. He keeps his nose to the ground, sniffing it carefully. He wears a harness attached to a long string. The grass is brown and Samo is brown, too. His handlers can hardly see him. They use the string to follow Samo's path. Suddenly Samo stops. He scratches at the ground. His handlers come up carefully behind him. Samo has found a hidden bomb called a land mine!

"Good job, Samo!" Samo's handler calls him back for his reward—a tasty piece of banana. Samo loves bananas. That's because he's an African giant pouched rat.

Bart Weetjens smiles proudly at the squirrel-size rat. He has worked very hard to bring his rats to this African minefield. Bart remembers how just 15 years ago, people laughed at his idea to use rats to find land mines. After all, who would believe that rats could be useful working animals? They aren't strong and fast like a horse, or brave and loyal like a dog. They don't have abilities like dolphins, which are sometimes trained to find bombs underwater. But rats are pretty special. They are smart and easy to train. They don't mind doing simple tasks over and over. And they have a great sense of smell.

Most people see rats as a pest. But Bart saw something great: the chance to solve a global problem—land mines. Millions of land mines are hidden on or under the ground in nearly 80 countries around the world. That's more than one in every three countries. The bombs are left over from wars. Sometimes they are hard to see when they are covered by a thin layer of dirt or grass. If someone steps on a mine, it can explode. The devices cause thousands of injuries and deaths every year.

Bart knew that people could never be safe with such deadly weapons around. The land mines had to go. But how? Finding land mines is dangerous and difficult. Many people have tried different ways to do it. Each method has problems. What could Bart try that hadn't been done before? To find an answer, Bart thought back to his childhood in Belgium and a little hamster named Goldy, who started his love for rodents.

"Happy birthday, Bart!"

Bart's mom and dad had opened the door to his room. His dad carried a small cage wrapped in ribbon.

"What's this?" Bart shouted, running to the cage.

A shaggy-haired hamster poked his head out. Bart reached in and scooped up the golden ball of fur.

"Wow, he's so soft and cute. I'll name him Goldy after the color of his hair. Thanks, Mom and Dad!"

"You have to take care of him yourself, Bart," said Bart's mom.

"That's right," agreed his dad. "Goldy is your responsibility."

"I promise I will. You won't have to worry about a thing."

Bart kept his promise to his parents and took care of Goldy's every need. The two were never apart. Bart kept Goldy in the pocket of his shirt. Sometimes, Goldy snoozed in the crook of his arm. Bart took Goldy along when he went to play with his friends. He and Goldy went shopping in the supermarket. He even took Goldy to school!

No one knows I have a hamster hidden in my clothes, Bart thought to himself. It was like he and Goldy shared a secret.

It wasn't long before Bart's secret got out. Bart was in trouble.

"Bart, I'm glad that you and Goldy are so close. But you can't take him out of the house. It's not safe for him," Bart's mom told him. She knew that if Goldy got away, the little fur ball would be really hard to find.

Bart agreed to leave Goldy at home from then on. But he worried that his buddy would get lonely. Bart wondered if he could get a friend for Goldy. His parents said he could. Soon after the

Did You Know?

African giant rats have pouches in their cheeks like hamsters that they use to store food.

new hamster came, baby hamsters were born.

Bart's parents didn't want a dozen little Goldys running around the house. They told Bart he would have to find a new home for the babies once they were big enough to leave their mom.

Bart took the young hamsters to a pet store. To his surprise, the shopkeeper gave him some money for each hamster.

This is great! thought Bart. *If Goldy has more babies, I can have fun and make money, too!*

The shopkeeper said Bart could also sell him other baby animals. Before long, a row of cages lined a wall of Bart's room. Inside, hamsters, gerbils, squirrels, and rats ran around happily.

Bart's parents were a little nervous about having so many rodents in the house. But Bart cleaned the animals' cages. He gave his rodents fresh food and water every day. He played with them and petted them. Since the hobby made their son so happy, Bart's parents allowed it.

Rats became Bart's favorite of all. They were so smart and friendly! Plus, they had an amazing sense of smell.

I bet rats could do lots of cool things, Bart thought.

At age 14, Bart left home to go to boarding school. He had to leave his rodent friends behind. Little did Bart know that when he grew up, rats would be part of his life again. This time, the stakes would be higher. Bart was going to use rats to save lives.

Giant Rats

African giant pouched rats can be found in many parts of Africa. They weigh 2 to 3 pounds (0.9 to 1.4 kg) and can grow up to 3 feet (0.9 m) long (including their tail). In the wild, they're active at night and sleep during the day.

While this type of rat is social and easy to train, they don't make very good pets. The animals have a strong chewing instinct. They'll chew on anything they find in your house.

Land mines like this one are a very serious problem all over the world.

AN EXPLOSIVE PROBLEM

It was 1995. A war had ended in Mozambique, a country in Africa. Both sides had used land mines. They buried the small bombs under dirt or leaves. When a person stepped on one of the mines, it would blow up. When a car ran over one, it would explode. Some mines were buried to keep the enemy away. Others were used to scare the enemy.

When the war was over, the killing stopped, right? No, it didn't. The mines were still there. People stepped on them and were hurt or killed. Farmers ran over them while plowing their fields. Kids stepped on them when playing ball.

Mozambique is not the only country with land mines. About 100 million mines are buried all over the world. They kill or hurt thousands of people each year. This is a very big problem.

Since the war ended, many countries have agreed to stop using land mines. They have also agreed to get rid of the land mines they have. But there is still one big problem: How do you get rid of the land mines that are already buried in the ground?

Many people have tried to solve this problem but have not been successful. This is mostly because finding the land mines is dangerous and very expensive. The problem had gotten so bad that people were beginning to lose hope.

Bart knew all of this, and he wanted to help. He read what other people had written about finding land mines. Many people had ideas on how to get rid of mines. One group used a high-tech sensor to find them. Another made a machine that could see mines in the dirt. These ideas didn't work very well. They needed electricity, and mines are often in places that don't have electricity.

Other people had made special cars. These cars had armor to keep them safe when a mine exploded. But they only worked on flat land. Metal detectors weren't right either. They found every piece of metal on the ground. They found some mines, but they found mostly coins and rusty screws.

Dogs were trained to sniff out TNT, the stuff that makes land mines explode. But sometimes the dog would set off the bomb and be hurt or killed. No one wants a dog to be hurt. The dogs got sick a lot, too. People realized this idea wasn't a good solution either.

Bart needed a new way to find land mines quickly and well. He knew that it had to be simple and not cost a lot of money. One day, he read an article about scientists who trained gerbils to find bombs. He thought back to the rats he had kept as pets when he was young. They were smarter than gerbils, and they had a great sense of smell. *That's it!* he thought. The idea struck him like a lightning bolt.

Rats can do that! I'll train African rats to sniff out mines. They're too small to explode the mines because they don't weigh enough. Their lives won't be at risk. Plus, they don't cost too much to feed. They can't get sick from local diseases because they are already used to them. And they are easy to take wherever they need to go.

Bart typed a letter. He sent it to a group that gives money to projects that help the world. The group told him they didn't like his idea. They didn't give him any money. Bart sent the letter to another group and then another. Almost two years passed, and still no group thought Bart's idea would work.

Finally, in 1997, someone liked his idea. The Belgian government gave him the money he needed to test it. Bart set up a training program. He had to make his rats ready for the hard work in the minefields. Only then could Bart's rats become the heroes he hoped they would be.

Bart chose the African giant pouched rat for his project. These rats live an average of six to eight years. They're calm, friendly, and easy to handle. Plus, with their large size, they're easier to spot in thick grass than smaller rats.

Bart got the idea to use the pouched rat from a friend. When his friend was in Africa, he saw a person walking one on a leash.

This is the rat for us! Bart thought when he found out about it.

Bart's training program starts soon after the rats are born. At five weeks old, the rats are ready to leave their mother. People take care of them for one to two weeks so the rats get used to being around humans. Each rat is given a name. Then, it's time to start the training.

The rat trainers teach the rats to do simple tricks. When a rat does a good job, the trainer gives it a food treat. At the same time, the trainer makes a clicking sound. The rat learns that a click means it has done a good job and will get a treat.

The trainers teach the rats to find TNT by its smell. At "sniff school," rats go into a large tank with slots along the bottom. Scents are loaded into the slots.

A rat runs along the bottom of the tank, its nose to the ground. When it stops at the TNT scent, CLICK . . . Snack time! The rat gets a bit of banana or a peanut each time it finds the TNT smell.

The training is repeated until the rats learn to stop and scratch at the spot where they smell TNT. From start to finish, the training program takes from eight to twelve months. Some rats learn fast and some learn slowly. Bart's rats seemed to be getting the hang of it pretty quickly.

Rat Athletes

Talk about a rat race! At a college in Nebraska, rats compete in events like the long jump, tightrope walk, rope climb, and weight lifting. It's like the Olympic Games for rats!

Students train the rats as part of a science class. When the rats learn a step to a trick, they're rewarded with goodies like protein pellets or yogurt chips. Eventually, the behaviors are combined into a complete skill.

A rat is rewarded with a chunk of banana for a job well done.

RATS TO THE RESCUE

Bart's rats practiced for months until they were expert TNT finders. Bart knew that they were ready for the next step: It was time to go outside. Bart set up a fake minefield. He buried old mines that were fixed so they couldn't explode. The mines still had bits of TNT for the rats to sniff out. They were great for the rats to practice on.

Pouched rats aren't used to being in the sun. They usually only come out at night. Bart made sure to protect them. The scientists put sunscreen in the rats' ears.

The rats scampered over the grass. They found all the TNT smells. Bart knew they were ready to be heroes. Now it was time for them to find real land mines. In 2008 and 2009, Bart's company, HeroRats, sent 30 rats to sniff more than 600 square miles (1,500 sq km) of land in Mozambique. The rats found 400 land mines! They did such a good job that they got a new goal. The government asked HeroRats to find all the land mines in the country by 2014.

Bart knew his rats could do it. Every day, he sees how the rats have helped people.

In 2010, HeroRats was sent to a village where the electric company couldn't work. There were mines hidden where they needed to put wires. Many people had no electricity for cooking or refrigeration. Children couldn't study at night because they didn't have lights. They couldn't use electronics like computers or televisions.

Bart's HeroRats found 40 mines in the small minefield. A team came to destroy the mines. The area was safe for the electric company workers.

When Bart visited the village later, he saw how much it had changed. Now the village had electricity. There were new schools, stores, and places for people to work. The villagers had a better life—and it was all thanks to HeroRats.

Meet the Rats

Each HeroRat has its own name and personality. Here are a few of the program's most famous critters.

ANZO

Bart's favorite rat lived to be nine years old. That's very, very old for a rat. She had so many babies that lots of today's HeroRats are Anzo's grandchildren and great-grandchildren.

ARARAT

Ararat was
HeroRats' star student.
He breezed through the
training program. Bart sent
him to Mozambique right away. If there's
a land mine around, Ararat will find it.

GRIGORY

Grigory isn't a top student, but he tries
hard. During his field training,
he missed a fake mine.
But Grigory's trainer
isn't ready to give up
on him. "Tomorrow,
he'll know he needs
to do better."

At another village, mines had been buried in a field next to a school. Teachers and students feared that one step could bring disaster. Children could not go outside at recess. They had to be careful on their way home from school.

The HeroRats were called in to sniff out the land mines. They cleared the whole area—finding more than 100 mines! Now, children can play safely in the schoolyard. They can have recess and play soccer and tag.

Bart and his rats have come a long way. They are still working in Mozambique. Now they clear land mines in neighboring Tanzania too. The group is planning to go to Thailand, a country in Asia where many mines are buried. They're also beginning another important job.

Some scientists thought that if these rats were so good at finding bombs, they might be good at finding other things too. As luck would have it, they are. These rats are now finding an illness called tuberculosis (sounds like TOO-BURR-CUE-LOW-SIS).

Tuberculosis, also called TB, mostly attacks people's lungs. It is a big problem all over the world. When someone has TB, he or she can give it to other people by sneezing or coughing.

> **Did You Know?**
>
> Rats are not the only animals that can sniff for deadly disease. Some dogs have been trained to find cancer using their sense of smell.

In the United States, TB is not very common. In Africa, many people have this illness. In many cases, it can be deadly.

The good news is that there is medicine to treat people with TB. The bad news is that it costs a lot of money to test people for the disease. But HeroRats can help! When a person has TB, a certain kind of germ is found in their spit. The germ has a scent. And as Bart's rats have proved, rats are very good at picking out scents.

Scientists started training the HeroRats to sniff for the TB germ. They did this the same way they trained the rats to sniff for land mines. They put different samples of spit into a tank with holes in the bottom. The rats would wander over the holes. When they smelled the TB scent, they would stop for a few seconds. If they were correct, they received a banana or a peanut. Pretty soon the rats learned to pass by the holes where they didn't smell TB. They went straight for the holes that smelled like the germ—and got the reward!

Once the rats were trained, doctors put them to the test. They found out that the rats aren't just as good as expensive tests— they're even better! They find almost twice as many TB cases as the tests do.

The testing with rats is still in the beginning stages. Scientists have more work to do before the test can be used on real people. Still, they are hopeful that the rats could one day be the number one test for TB. If the rats are as good at finding the illness as some people think they are, they may save a lot of lives.

HeroRats is not alone in working to solve the problems of land mines or tuberculosis. Many people around the world are helping, and it is paying off. In 2002, almost 12,000 people around the world were killed or hurt in land mine accidents. Now, that number is less than 4,200 a year. In 2011, the number of TB cases went down for the first time in years.

Bart knows there is still work to do. But with his rats' help, the world is already a better place.

THE END

INDEX

MORE INFORMATION

To find more information about the animal species featured in this book, check out these books and websites:

Face to Face With Dolphins,
National Geographic, 2007

National Geographic Kids Everything Dolphins,
National Geographic, 2012

Rain Forest Alliance "Kid's Corner: Capuchin Monkey"
www.rainforest-alliance.org/kids/species-profiles/capuchin-monkey

National Geographic Digital Motion Rat Genius (video)
www.natgeoeducationvideo.com/film/283/rat-genius

National Geographic Channel "Capuchin Monkey" (short video)
natgeotv.com.au/videos/animals/capuchin-monkey-CF3958F9.aspx

This book is dedicated to the human heroes: Ned Sullivan, Chris Blankenship, and Bart Weetjens. Thank you for sharing your inspiring stories and making our world a better place.

CREDITS

Inside This Book title page (in order of books, top to bottom): courtesy of Ellen Rogers; Lieve Blancquaert; courtesy of Carolina Tiger Rescue; Title page, Shawn Jackson/Dreamstime.com; 4, Jason Nuttle; 6, Tony Ashby/AFP/Getty Images; 12 (LE), Flukeprint/Dreamstime.com; 12 (RT), Shawn Jackson/Dreamstime.com; 16, Jason Nuttle; 23, Amidala76/Shutterstock; 26, Bill Sumner; 33, New England Aquarium; 36, Ivan de Petrovski; 38, Courtesy of Ellen Rogers; 45, Osebeck/Dreamstime.com; 48, Courtesy of Ellen Rogers; 57, Vilainecrevette/Dreamstime.com; 58, Courtesy of Ellen Rogers; 67, Courtesy of Ellen Rogers; 68, Stuart Franklin/Magnum Photos; 70, Alvaro Laiz; 79, David Rengel; 80, Stuart Franklin/Magnum Photos; 89, William Lauer/Lincoln Journal Star; 90, Stuart Franklin/Magnum Photos; 94, Alvaro Laiz; 95 (UP), Lieve Blancquaert; 95 (LO), APOPO; 102, Shawn Jackson/Dreamstime.com

ACKNOWLEDGMENTS

Elizabeth Carney would like to acknowledge the following organizations for helping to make this book possible:

APOPO and HeroRats
www.apopo.org

The Dolphin and Marine Medical Research Foundation
www.dmmr.org

Helping Hands
www.monkeyhelpers.org

Book 3

TIGER IN TROUBLE!

And More True Stories of Amazing Animal Rescues

Kelly Milner Halls

Published by the National Geographic Society
John M. Fahey, Jr., *Chairman of the Board and Chief Executive Officer*
Timothy T. Kelly, *President*
Declan Moore, *Executive Vice President; President, Publishing and Digital Media*
Melina Gerosa Bellows, *Executive Vice President; Chief Creative Officer, Books, Kids, and Family*

Prepared by the Book Division
Hector Sierra, *Senior Vice President and General Manager*
Nancy Laties Feresten, *Senior Vice President, Editor in Chief, Children's Books*
Jonathan Halling, *Design Director, Books and Children's Publishing*
Jay Sumner, *Director of Photography, Children's Publishing*
Jennifer Emmett, *Editorial Director, Children's Books*
Eva Absher-Schantz, *Managing Art Director, Children's Books*
Carl Mehler, *Director of Maps*
R. Gary Colbert, *Production Director*
Jennifer A. Thornton, *Director of Managing Editorial*

Staff for This Book
Becky Baines and Laura F. Marsh, *Project Editors*
Lori Epstein, *Illustrations Editor*
Eva Absher-Schantz, *Art Director*
YAY! Design, *Designer*
Grace Hill, *Associate Managing Editor*
Joan Gossett, *Production Editor*
Lewis R. Bassford, *Production Manager*
Susan Borke, *Legal and Business Affairs*
Kate Olesin, *Assistant Editor*
Kathryn Robbins, *Design Production Assistant*
Hillary Moloney, *Illustrations Assistant*

Manufacturing and Quality Management
Phillip L. Schlosser, *Senior Vice President*
Chris Brown, *Vice President, NG Book Manufacturing*
George Bounelis, *Vice President, Production Services*
Nicole Elliott, *Manager*
Rachel Faulise, *Manager*
Robert L. Barr, *Manager*

For more information, please call 1-800-NGS LINE (647-5463) or write to the following address:
National Geographic Society
1145 17th Street N.W.
Washington, D.C. 20036-4688 U.S.A.

Visit us online at nationalgeographic.com/books

For librarians and teachers: ngchildrensbooks.org

National Geographic supports K–12 educators with ELA Common Core Resources. Visit natgeoed.org/commoncore for more information.

More for kids from National Geographic:
kids.nationalgeographic.com

For information about special discounts for bulk purchases, please contact National Geographic Books Special Sales: ngspecsales@ngs.org

For rights or permissions inquiries, please contact National Geographic Books Subsidiary Rights: ngbookrights@ngs.org

Trade paperback ISBN: 978-1-4263-1078-2
Reinforced library edition ISBN:
978-1-4263-1079-9

Table of CONTENTS

Nitro, a 600-pound tiger, is cared for by Carolina Tiger Rescue.

NITRO: TIGER IN TROUBLE

Nitro's Kansas home was a tiny cage in a junkyard.

Ten-year-old Nitro paced in his cage. It was the evening of February 21, 2009. The sun was setting quickly. Nitro's owner, Jeffrey Harsh, was late with the tiger's dinner.

Hungry big cats get restless, but Nitro couldn't pace far. His chain-link cage was only 20 feet wide and 30 feet long—one-third the size of a school gym. Nitro was eight feet long. He could only take a few steps. Then he had to turn and walk the other way. Back and forth. Back and forth.

He stepped over bones in the dust. They were left over from earlier meals. He brushed against Apache, the other tiger in his cage. His empty belly grumbled. He growled and roared.

Nitro and Apache were not alone. There were three female lions in other cages nearby. All of these big cats were living at the Prairie Cat Animal Refuge near Oakley, Kansas—and they were all hungry.

A man wandered to the main gate. The cats' eyes locked on him. He opened the gate and slowly came inside.

The man passed piles of junk.

He looked into each animal's cage. Nitro listened, while the other cats studied the stranger.

Then the man walked toward a lioness. He slipped his hand inside the metal bars of her gate.

It was a very bad choice.

To the hungry lion, his arm looked like dinner. Her instinct told her to catch her meal, and she listened. She bit down on the stranger's arm. He screamed and screamed.

Just then Jeffrey drove up with a truck full of meat. He could tell right away things were not right. The entry gate was unlocked and open. Screams were coming from the big cats' cages. Jeffrey jumped out of his truck and ran toward the sound.

Jeffrey saw the stranger. He ran past

Nitro, toward the lion cage. Jeffrey grabbed the man and tried to pull him free. But he wasn't as strong as the lion, and she would not let go. He never hit the animals, but he didn't know what else to do. The man was in serious danger.

Jeffrey picked up a metal pipe and swung at the lioness. At last, she opened her jaws, and the frightened man fell back. Jeffrey rushed the stranger to the hospital. As he drove, he called the police on his cell phone.

Nitro would have to wait a little longer for his dinner. His owner was under arrest. He had not protected the stranger from the dangerous big cats.

Until that night, Jeffrey Harsh had broken no laws. Almost half of the states in the U.S. have passed laws to make it illegal to own wild animals like Nitro. Thirteen other states have some rules that say who can keep them and who cannot. The rest of the states have almost no laws at all. There, almost anyone can buy a wild animal.

Kansas is one of the 13 states with some rules. But the rules are not strong enough, said Sheriff Rod Taylor, the officer who arrested Jeffrey. Owners do not even need to take a class to learn how to care for a wild animal. If people like Jeffrey Harsh follow a few rules, they can buy big cats and raise them. And terrible things can happen.

Jeffrey didn't see it that way. He didn't think his big cats would hurt anyone.

He thought since his animals were raised in captivity, or in cages, they would not act like wild animals.

"They were born in captivity," he said on his website, "and bottle fed, so they think they are human. They are as gentle and sweet as a house cat." He was wrong.

The judge gave Jeffrey a choice. He could pay fines and spend months in jail, or he could give the big cats to people who knew how to take care of them. Jeffrey decided to give his pets away. The lionesses were headed to the Detroit Zoo. But this zoo didn't need any tigers. No zoo did.

Did You Know?

Every tiger has stripes, but not all stripes are alike. In fact, none of them are. No two tigers have exactly the same pattern.

So You Think You Want a Baby Tiger?

Keeping a baby tiger as a pet might seem like a great idea. At first, they weigh only a few pounds. And they don't have teeth. They are cute and harmless.

But as they grow bigger and stronger, tigers play rough. They can hurt their owners. It is better to visit a tiger in a zoo or animal rescue. They don't belong in people's homes.

So where would Nitro and Apache go?

Sheriff Taylor called animal rescue experts for help. They told him about Carolina Tiger Rescue in North Carolina. Would they agree to take Nitro and Apache? That was the big question.

Kathryn Bertok works at Carolina Tiger Rescue. She takes care of the animals that live there.

"We won't take an animal unless we can take them for the rest of their lives," Kathryn explained. That's because moving a tiger is hard. It is hard for the tiger. It is also hard for the people moving it.

Tigers that are cared for by humans can live to be 20 years old. Nitro and Apache were 10 years old. Tiger Rescue would have to pay the cost of feeding and

caring for two tigers for ten more years.
Could they afford it?

There was another important question:
How much space would Nitro and Apache
need? Big cats get sad in small spaces. They
pace in a figure-eight pattern. They pant
and grumble. They even suck their tails,
like a baby human sucks its thumb.

The tiny cage in Kansas was far too
small for two full-grown cats. A new home
for Nitro and Apache would need to be
bigger. Much bigger. It would take a space
37 times as big as their Kansas cage to
keep them happy.

Experts at Carolina Tiger Rescue
thought long and hard.

At last, they answered yes.

The experts at Carolina Tiger Rescue know how to care for and move big cats.

Chapter 2

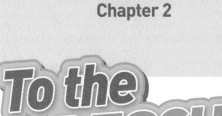

To the RESCUE

Moving Nitro and Apache from Kansas to North Carolina would be a tiger-size challenge. Even so, Kathryn was sure she could do it.

Kathryn loaded the Rescue's truck. She put in two large crates— one for Nitro and one for Apache. She also took along tools and fence cutters. The tiger cubs had grown large in their little chain-link cage.

They were now too big to get in and out through the door. Kathryn might have to cut the cage apart.

On April 12, 2009, Kathryn arrived in Oakley, Kansas. She had been driving for 26 hours. She checked into a hotel and got ready for a good night's sleep. Saving two tigers would not be easy. Kathryn would need all her strength and energy.

Kathryn, Sheriff Taylor, and an animal doctor called a veterinarian (vet) met at the front gate of the Prairie Cat Animal Refuge. Nitro was awake. He heard new voices and smelled unfamiliar scents. The strangers made him feel uneasy. He paced and softly grumbled.

Kathryn could tell that the tigers were calm. But they did not seem to trust her.

"Animals can sense when something big is about to happen," she said.

It was time for Nitro and Apache to take a nap. The vet had a special dart gun to shoot medicine into the tigers. If the darts hit just right, Nitro and Apache would be fast asleep in no time. They would sleep while the team moved them. Then they would wake up safe and sound inside their travel crates. The vet knew just the right amount of medicine to use.

POP. POP. The vet pulled the trigger, and the darts hit their targets.

Nitro hissed quietly when the dart hit his shoulder. His ears fell flat against his head. He was afraid. Then he felt the medicine start to work. He settled down. His stomach was flat on the dusty earth.

His breathing slowed down. He fell into a deep and peaceful sleep.

Quickly, Kathryn cut a large hole in the chain-link fence. She and the others climbed through the hole into the cage. Gently, they loaded Nitro into a large travel crate. It looked like a crate for a very large dog.

Nitro woke a short time later. He was safely loaded into the Carolina Tiger Rescue truck. Kathryn drove east, out of Kansas. Nitro was slightly confused, but not afraid.

"It depends on the animal," Kathryn said. "But these guys were fine. When you get on the road, they tend to settle down, like kids. The movement of the truck relaxes them."

Every two hours, Nitro saw his new caretakers. They stopped to check on him and give him food or water. Twenty-six hours later, Nitro was at the rescue. But it would still be another month before he could move into his forever home.

The concrete cells where Nitro and Apache first stayed weren't very comfortable. The hard surface felt strange against Nitro's paws. But the cells were clean and safe.

The people at the rescue needed to keep Nitro and Apache separated. They could not be near the other cats for 30 days. During that time, the tigers would get a full medical checkup by the veterinarians.

If they had any diseases, the vets could find out before they passed it on to other tigers. They would also check Nitro and Apache for injuries and give them medicine if they needed it. Only after that could the tigers be around other animals.

The veterinarian put Nitro to sleep again. This time, it was a much deeper sleep because the vet had a lot to do. Nitro needed his teeth cleaned. He had to get shots. And he needed to have a tiny microchip placed just under his skin. Then he could be tracked and returned to Carolina Tiger Rescue if he was ever lost or stolen.

How Much Does a Captive Tiger Eat?

Some wild tigers can eat 40 pounds of meat each day. Others can gobble down as much as 70 pounds.

Tigers in the wild are more active than tigers in captivity. They hunt for miles. Wild tigers also eat a lot when they can because weeks can pass between meals.

At Carolina Tiger Rescue, the diet is different. Tigers eat smaller meals—15 to 20 pounds of meat. Also, they eat five days a week. Nitro eats whole chickens, beef, goats, and deer.

"It's not pretty," Kathryn said. "But it's important to their health."

When most big cats wake up, they are a little sleepy, but otherwise healthy. Nitro was not most big cats.

As he woke, Nitro began to moan and pant. He could hardly stand, and he was confused. Kathryn had seen it before—Nitro was suffering from hyperthermia (sounds like hi-per-THUR-mee-uh). That meant he could not control his body temperature. His fever was rising quickly. If the staff didn't act fast to cool him, he might not survive.

Kathryn brought out water hoses. Each animal caretaker took turns bathing Nitro's body with cool water. They needed to keep his fever down. "His paws went bright pink when he was in trouble," she said. "Keeping him cool really helped."

After two days, Nitro was finally getting better. He was hungry. He even started to walk around his cage. But Kathryn noticed something strange.

Three of the four walls of the cage were made of concrete. The fourth wall was made of chain link. Most animals faced the chain-link wall. They like to watch what is going on outside of their cage. Nitro did not.

"He would sit and stare at the concrete walls," Kathryn said. "And when he did turn toward our voices, he would follow the sound of our voices. But not our movements."

Kathryn knew this meant one thing: Nitro was blind.

Caretakers at the
Tiger Rescue thought
of ways to help blind
Nitro find his way
around his cage.

Chapter 3

Now that he was healthy, Nitro was ready for his new cage. But he couldn't see it. His owner in Kansas had never noticed Nitro was blind. That cage had been so small, Nitro had been able to memorize every inch. So, he may not have seemed blind.

Why was Nitro blind? That's hard to tell.

Kathryn ruled out a brain injury.

And there were no scars around Nitro's eyes that might mean he had an injury. "We just don't know what caused his condition," Kathryn said.

Here's what they did know. The caretakers at the Rescue had a big challenge ahead of them. They had to help a blind tiger find his way, without the use of his eyes.

Nitro walked through his big new home. He reached out with huge six-inch paws. He was trying to feel what was ahead of him. He did not know where things were around him. Not a twig, not a path, not a feeding dish.

He was a little afraid. He could never tell when he was getting close to running into the fence.

"He was roughing up his nose, because he would walk right up to the fence and hit it," Kathryn said. "We kept thinking, 'you have to slow down.'" But how do you teach a blind tiger how to find a fence he cannot see?

"We decided to start marking the fence with peppermint," Kathryn explained. "He would know when he smelled it, he should slow down. The peppermint marked the borders of his space."

Once he learned where his fences were, the people at the Rescue put down sand pathways. The sand pathways led to Nitro's food, water, and his cozy den.

When Nitro felt sand under his paws, he knew he would end up in one of those areas. When Nitro felt leaves, dirt, and twigs, he knew he was not heading in the right direction.

In time, Nitro learned where every bump, every tree, and every food box was in his new cage. When he did, the sand and the peppermint could be put away. Nitro was finally home.

Caretakers noticed a big change in Nitro. He mastered his space. He couldn't see people. But he knew where they were, even if they stood perfectly still.

He chuffled in their direction to get them to answer. He wanted to hear if he knew their voices. He wanted to know who they were.

Nitro, the blind tiger, has become a Rescue favorite. Volunteers guide people through Carolina Tiger Rescue once a week. They never miss a stop at Nitro's cage. They tell his story and give him little treats (scraps of chicken or beef). Nitro never disappoints.

"He has a great attitude," Kathryn says. "Things haven't been easy for him. But he still comes up to the fence happily chuffling."

Caretakers agree. Nitro is a trusting tiger. He never seems cranky or mad. Even so, he was and still is a tough, wild tiger. He still has his kill instincts.

In many ways, Nitro acts like a pet cat. He takes catnaps. He scratches his claws on trees, like a house cat would use a scratching post. He rolls in the dirt. He licks his fur to groom himself. He likes to play by crouching and then pouncing.

Still, Nitro's size and weight would make those playful swats and scratches deadly. If a house cat gets scared and claws your hand, you need a bandage. If a tiger gets scared and uses its claws, you could get a cut that needs stitches. Or something worse.

The tiger isn't "turning mean." It's showing behavior that keeps it alive in the wild.

In the wild, tigers are solitary animals, which means they live alone. They need to protect themselves and find food. Their keen eyes notice even the smallest movements. They pounce with their powerful legs. Tigers hold the animals they catch tightly, so they can't get away. They kill the animals quickly. Then they defend the food they catch with sharp claws, so other tigers won't steal it.

Tigers at zoos or rescues do not need to use the rough behavior tigers use in the wild. Tigers in captivity don't need to find their own food. And they won't be attacked by other animals.

But in captivity or in the wild, tigers have the same kill instincts.

Creating more laws to help big cats would stop some unhappy endings for tigers like Nitro. If every state makes owning tigers against the law, only zoos and special programs could raise them.

Fewer animals would be mistreated or killed.

Nitro, the tiger in trouble, will be safe from now on. He spends his days wandering around his huge cage. He naps in his den, and he trots toward people who visit him. He roars at the other cats in the rescue, and they answer him. Nitro is happy, and he is loved.

The people at Carolina Tiger Rescue will take care of him for the rest of his life. Even Nitro can "see" how great that ending turned out to be.

Kids Can Help

Here are some ideas to help big cats like Nitro:

- Organize a penny drive: Set up jars or cans at school. Ask people to donate their pennies. Send the money to a big cat rescue group.

- Sponsor a big cat: Families or classrooms can sponsor a big cat at Carolina Tiger Rescue. This helps pay for its care.

- Learn about National Geographic's Big Cat Initiative at animals.national geographic.com/animals/big-cats/about.

- Support countries that protect tigers and their habitats by visiting there.

Learn more about Carolina Tiger Rescue at www.carolinatigerrescue.org.

Bats at rest fold their delicate wings close to their bodies.

ETHEREAL: AN ALBINO BAT BABY

There are about 1,000 species of bats in the world. Ethereal is a Mexican free-tailed bat.

Chapter 1

LOST and FOUND

The tiny bat was hungry. She had to go hunting for something to eat. But she knew she was taking a chance.

She soared into the Texas air. She needed to catch enough insects to stay alive. She liked all kinds of insects. There were moths, dragonflies, beetles, and many others. But other animals were also hunting. She needed to be careful.

Her pink wings spread. They lifted her tiny body high into the night sky.

She was a Mexican free-tailed bat. This kind of bat is one of the fastest animals in the world. She had no trouble darting and weaving.

She sent out sound waves. Each one bounced back to tell her what was ahead. They also told her where she might find her next meal. She was using echolocation (sounds like eck-oh-low-KAY-shun).

Sometimes, the sound waves told her she was near something too big to eat. It might be a tree branch or a big animal. Sometimes, the sound waves said she was near something too small to be a tasty bug. Sometimes, the waves were just right. Then she knew she was close to something yummy and just her size.

The little bat found a flying June bug, and she dived toward the juicy snack. Moonlight shone on her fur. She was easy to see against the pitch-black sky.

She zipped and zoomed toward her meal. But she was not the only one looking for dinner.

Just then a barn owl swooped out of the darkness. He flew full speed toward the tiny bat. His sharp claws opened as he moved in toward her small body.

The bat used every trick she knew to escape. Hunting would have to wait. She changed direction. She flew toward an old house below her.

Heart pounding, she sailed through the open window. She landed on the wooden rafters and tried to catch her breath.

Blending in was just too hard, no matter how she tried. The tiny bat had albinism (sounds like AL-been-iz-um), which made her fur white.

With no brown color, the little white bat looked like a tiny angel. She moved, inch by inch, across the beams. She was tired and weak. And now she would have another night without food. The poor bat was starving.

But she was in luck. It would be her last hungry night. The old house she flew into was owned by Bat World Sanctuary.

Bat World Sanctuary rescues and protects bats. The staff also teach people about bats. The starving little bat had found just the right place to rest.

What Is Albinism?

Ethereal has albinism. This means that her body does not make pigment. Pigment adds color to skin, hair, and eyes. It also protects skin from the sun.

What causes albinism? It's an accident of nature. It doesn't happen very often. Most parents of albino babies are not albinos themselves. They usually have typical coloring.

Most animals with albinism don't see very well. But echolocation helped the little white bat hunt without using her eyes.

Many thousands of Mexican free-tailed bats were living in the old home. They slept during the day. They huddled together to keep warm. As many as 500 baby bats or 200 adult bats dangled from each square foot of the ceiling. The places where they hung are called roosts. At night, they flew out to hunt for insects.

The people at Bat World were studying the huge group of bats living there. Bats are the only flying mammals on Earth. Mammals have fur and give birth to their young. Mammal babies also drink their mother's milk. Unlike birds, baby bats drink milk until they are old enough to hunt for bugs on their own.

Staff members would leave their main office every few days to check for wounded bats. This is especially important in June and July, when new bat pups are born.

Owls and hawks eat young Mexican free-tailed bats. Snakes, raccoons, and house cats do, too. If young bats fall from their high roosts, the mother bats do not rescue them. People at Bat World rescue them instead.

Amanda Lollar is the director of Bat World. She is the person who discovered the little white bat the next day. "When we saw her 15 feet above us, she stood out like a spotlight," Amanda said.

Usually, Amanda and her team take rescued bats to their main office. They don't plan to keep them forever. They hope to make them healthy. Then they release them into the Texas sky.

Bat rescue experts in Texas say albino Mexican free-tailed bats are seen only once every seven to ten years.

But this bat was different.

The bat was about eight weeks old. She had just stopped drinking her mother's milk. She was trying to hunt on her own. "But she hadn't been getting enough to eat," Amanda said. The tiny bat couldn't hunt enough to keep herself fed. She was so often hunted herself.

She had no dark color to blend into the dark night sky. The bat would never be able to live in the wild. Amanda decided to give her a new home. She would live at Bat World forever.

Volunteers from Bat World carefully caught the tiny white mammal. They gently placed her in a box. Then they drove her to their indoor sanctuary. There she got a complete checkup and a tasty dinner. Plus, she got a brand-new name—Ethereal (sounds like uh-THEE-ree-ul).

Why the name Ethereal? It means delicate or heavenly. "She was just so beautiful," Amanda said. "So otherworldly—like a little fairy. The name seemed to fit."

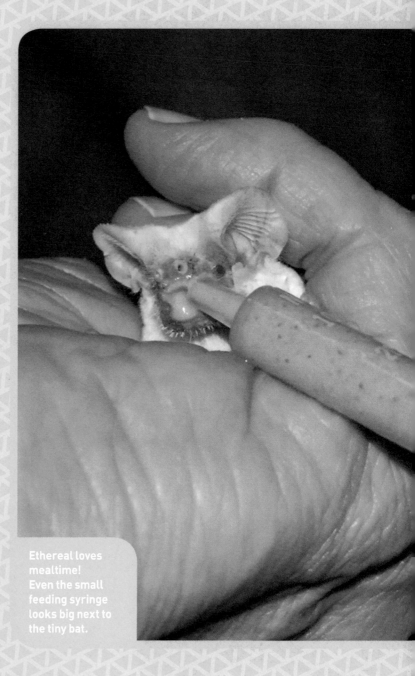

Ethereal loves mealtime! Even the small feeding syringe looks big next to the tiny bat.

Chapter 2

FOOD and Friendship

Like magic, Ethereal made friends with Amanda. "Bats are very smart," she said. "They may be as smart as dolphins. Ethereal knew we wanted to help her. She got used to us right away. She is a sweet, sweet little bat. Ethereal is shy with new people, but most bats are."

Close friendship is healthy for a bat. But being friends with just one person can be dangerous, too. That person might have to go away. A new person might come instead.

"If we don't prepare the bats for the change, they might stop eating," Amanda explained.

Food made the friendship between Amanda and Ethereal stronger. Like the bat's mother, Amanda was taking care of the little bat, and Ethereal knew it.

In the wild, Mexican free-tailed bats eat insects. Those insects eat flowers and fruits and vegetables. So, eating those bugs is a little like eating fruits and vegetables, too. The vitamins in those bugs make them good meals for bats.

Ethereal and the other bats at Bat World stay inside in huge rooms called flying cages. The bats can fly and play, chat and sleep, but they don't hunt for wild insects. Wild bugs aren't allowed in the flying cages because some could make the bats sick. So, Amanda makes healthy food for them.

"Bats that never really ate in the wild are given a soft food diet," Amanda said. "This includes mealworm guts."

The mealworms are full of vitamins and protein. They give bats lots of energy to swoop and soar. The Bat World workers use 200,000 mealworms every month to feed the bats.

Amanda makes sure every bat gets plenty to eat—just enough to make them healthy. But Ethereal has a favorite.

"She loves peaches," Amanda said.

"She's excited when peaches are in the mix." She slurps up the sticky stuff especially fast when her favorite food is served.

Some bats are fed food in feeding dishes. The dishes are piled high with mealworms and ripe fruits like berries and peaches. The bats gather at the dishes to eat.

Other bats like Ethereal are fed by hand. Volunteers measure vitamins, worm guts, fruit, and vegetables. Then they mash them up with a blender. Amanda fills a syringe (sounds like ser-INGE) with the tasty goo. It's dinner time!

One at a time, Amanda gathers each

bat into her left hand. She squeezes very carefully to hold it firmly. The bat puts its tiny, wrinkled lips on the syringe to eat.

With her right hand, Amanda slowly squirts the food into the bat's hungry mouth. The bat gobbles up the mixture. Amanda is very careful not to go too quickly. Too much food at one time could choke the bat. Also, she doesn't want to get food in the bat's tiny nose. When she's done, Amanda wipes each dirty little face.

It takes time to feed each bat by hand. But hand-feeding helps the bats learn to trust the caretakers.

Do the little bats like being hand fed? Amanda thinks so.

"At feeding times, we slip the bats into carriers. We call them 'bat huts,'" Amanda said. They move the bat huts filled with bats to the feeding room. If Amanda places the bat huts in the cages early, something amazing happens.

"They will load themselves into the bat huts," Amanda said. They know bat-hut time means mealtime!

Ethereal was not fed with the other bats at first. She was not allowed near any other animals. She was kept apart until Amanda knew she was healthy. If Ethereal were sick, she could make other bats sick, too.

Luckily, Ethereal was fine. The tiny bat's new life could begin. She had already started to eat better. She was getting her strength back.

More About Mexican Free-tailed Bats

In June, Mexican free-tailed bat mothers have tiny babies called pups. Each mother usually has one baby.

The mammal pup drinks its mother's milk. After it eats, the pup sleeps away from its mother. Hundreds of pups sleep together in one small space. Then the mothers leave to hunt for bugs.

How do mothers find their babies when they return? A mother can tell her pup by its voice and its familiar smell.

The next step was moving Ethereal to her new home. How bats live depends on what kind of bat they are.

"Tree bats live alone," Amanda said. "They mind their own business. Crevice bats are social. They get sad when they are alone."

"Ethereal is a crevice bat," Amanda said. "She needs friends."

Ethereal was placed in a cage with many other bats of her own kind. The other bats took a little getting used to.

So, Amanda gave Ethereal a safe place of her own—a basket on the floor of the huge cage. From the basket, she could watch the other bats. She could get out of the nest if she wanted to make new friends. She could stay in if she was feeling shy.

Amanda didn't rush Ethereal. She let her make friends when she was ready, so she wouldn't be afraid.

Soon Ethereal got used to the other bats. She spent more and more time playing with them. She chattered in little squeaks and clicks and hisses, and flew with them. She was learning more about them. She was becoming part of the colony.

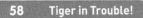

Amanda feeds Ethereal in her bat hut. The bat pokes her head out to ask for more dinner.

Chapter 3

Life in a NEW HOME

Ethereal was settling in. It was time to explore her new world. Then she would really feel at home.

Ethereal soared through the giant cage. She darted from corner to corner. She landed on dozens of roosts. She hung upside down. She could go anywhere. There were no hungry meat eaters in sight.

The other bats felt the same.

There were 150 bats in the colony. They dangled from the ceiling beside her. She fit right in. The other bats didn't seem to notice she wasn't the same color they were.

"In some species, other animals won't go near one that's different," Amanda said. "But Ethereal was accepted by the normal bats at Bat World."

Ethereal was getting to know the other bats. Every bat has its own personality and voice. "I study them," Amanda said, "And I've found at least 25 different sounds." That's like knowing 25 special bat words.

Amanda doesn't know what the bats are saying. But she does think they're talking with each other. She believes the bats put sounds together to have conversations. She thinks they may even make bat sentences. "I believe they are that smart," she said.

Ethereal settled right into the chatter. She even picked a ceiling roost of her very own.

"Ethereal lands in one spot almost every time," said Amanda. "She knows she is at home."

Making good friends was next on Ethereal's list. Which bats would be her pals? It took a few weeks to decide. She finally settled on a small group of female bats. She had found best friends of her very own.

How can you tell when bats are best friends? "They snuggle," Amanda said. "They chitter and peep and stay close together."

Ethereal chitters with three of the other girl bats most of the time. She likes Batzilla, Barbie, and Princess Ugly Toe.

The four girls get along great. But they do have little fights now and then. They chirp and chitter and fuss. Sometimes, they even hiss.

"It's like a soap opera," Amanda said with a laugh. But they really hang out. They actually dangle together, side by side.

Someday, Ethereal may have a mate. She may even have a pup of her own. "It's possible," said Amanda. "She's healthy. The boys treat her like all the other girls. They don't mind that she's an albino.

But for now, she doesn't seem interested. For now, she's happy as one of the girls."

That's okay, because Ethereal has an important job to do. She is teaching scientists about albino bats.

"We don't know much about albinism in bats," said Amanda. Studying Ethereal will help Bat World and other scientists understand albino bats a little better. Amanda will share all the facts she discovers.

Ethereal has another job to do. She teaches people who aren't scientists all about bats.

Ethereal goes to schools and community events. She is on the Bat World website. Many people get to meet her and learn more about her. They find out about all of the interesting things bats do—and what they don't do.

Some people think bats like to tangle themselves in human hair. But that's not true. Some people think all bats drink blood, but only South American vampire bats do. And vampire bats rarely try to drink human blood.

Other bat species do not drink blood at all. They eat fruit and insects—lots of insects. That is why farmers love bats. Insects damage the food farmers grow. So, when bats eat insects, they help keep farmers' crops safe. Ethereal can help Amanda and Bat World teach people the truth about bats.

Only five other bats at Bat World are friendly enough to do this work. Amanda said she chose Ethereal because she is so sweet. "I would never take a bat with me if it wasn't calm with people," she said. "It would be far too scary for the bat."

Bats also are sensitive. "You know how a cat can tell when someone doesn't like it?" Amanda said. "Bats are the same. If they sense you're trying to help them, they're friendly. If they think you don't really like bats, they act scared of you."

Amanda wants people to meet a sweet bat like Ethereal. Then they will realize what great animals bats are. Amanda has worked with bats for 20 years. She wants to stop other people from being scared of them. She hopes they will start seeing bats as friends.

Ethereal has a long life ahead of her.

A Mexican free-tailed bat can live 15 years in captivity.

"We had one orphan, named Andrea, who lived to be 19 years old," said Amanda. Ethereal might not live quite that long. But every day she is alive is a reason to be happy.

"She's such a little angel," Amanda said. "I hope she'll be happy and safe for a long, long time."

How Kids Can Help

It's never a good idea to keep a bat as a pet. But you can still help a flying mammal like Ethereal. Here's how:

You or your class can adopt a bat. Your donation provides food, medicine, and bat toys for a Bat World Sanctuary bat. You'll get a certificate, a photo, and regular updates on your bat.

To adopt a bat, visit Bat World Sanctuary at www.batworld.org/ adopt-a-bat-now.

If bats live where you live, you could build an outdoor bat house. The Bat Conservation International website tells you how. Visit www.batcon.org.

Suzie, Bob, and Caleb play well together at the Primate Rescue Center.

SUZIE, BOB, & CALEB: The Three Monkeyteers

Bob likes to wrestle and play. Vervet monkeys are good jumpers and climbers.

Chapter 1

ESCAPE From Tiny Cages

Could an old Olive baboon and two baby Vervet monkeys make a real family? Maybe not in the wild. But for Suzie, Bob, and Caleb, the weird mix worked. They found each other after tough times alone.

SUZIE

Suzie was very small when she was adopted more than 25 years ago. She weighed less than three pounds. She is an Olive baboon. She had thick black fur and a sweet pink face. Suzie was so cute. People smiled and laughed when they saw her.

The people who bought her didn't break the law. Keeping monkeys was allowed in their Kentucky neighborhood. But they probably didn't know how hard it was for the baboon.

"Babies are pulled from their mothers too soon," said Eileen Dunnington, an expert caretaker at the Primate Rescue Center. "This stops the mother-baby bonding. It is very hurtful to both the mother and baby."

Suzie's owners didn't think about that when they bought her. They thought of how much they would love her. They promised to care for Suzie forever.

Keeping the promise was easy when Suzie was little. Everything was easy when she was small. Her cage in the basement seemed so big. She was hardly ever in her cage because her owners wanted to play with her all the time. Owning a baby Olive baboon was fun.

Then Suzie started to grow.

Her black coat disappeared. The thick olive coat she was named for took its place. She gained weight quickly. In no time, she weighed 32 pounds.

She wasn't a tiny baby anymore. She was more than three feet long. Her cage seemed a whole lot smaller.

Once she wasn't a cute little baby, Suzie

got easier to ignore. Most of the time, Suzie was alone.

Being alone is hard for an Olive baboon. Monkeys like Suzie normally live in Africa, where it is loud and lively with wildlife. Baboon troops have 20 to 100 noisy members. They scamper together across the savannah.

Female troop leaders keep watch over dozens of Olive baboons of all ages. They hunt. They play. They groom one another. They even sleep together.

Did You Know?

Olive baboons live in more than 25 nations on the African continent.

Suzie slept and ate and daydreamed all by herself.

Food was also a problem for Suzie. In nature, she would have been an omnivore (sounds like OM-nee-vore). That means she would have gobbled up whatever food she could find. Her troop would have wandered for miles. They would have eaten grasses, roots, fruits, and insects. She might have even eaten birds or injured animals, if she was hungry enough.

Suzie's human family didn't have African fruits or vegetables. They didn't have insects or antelope, either. They fed her human food that wasn't healthy for a growing monkey.

Suzie grew fat because she had no way to exercise. She mostly stayed in her cage. She couldn't even stretch her restless, long legs.

Year after year, Suzie got sicker. And she became scared.

When Suzie turned 25 years old, her owners asked for help. They called the Primate Rescue Center in Nicholasville, Kentucky.

BOB

When Bob was born, he was an average little Vervet monkey. He was living with a private breeder.

The breeder raised baby monkeys for money. He sold them to strangers as pets. For some reason, no one wanted to buy Bob.

Bob was cute. He was only a few weeks old. He still had his light-colored baby face and blackish-colored fur. He weighed less than two pounds. He certainly had a lot of energy—too much energy maybe.

Bob got into everything when he was out of his cage. He climbed up curtains. He knocked things over. He didn't have sharp teeth yet. But crazy little Bob was quite a handful.

Weeks passed. The breeder needed Bob's cage for a new baby. So, the breeder's friend agreed to become Bob's foster mother. She took him home with her.

In the wilds of Africa, Bob would have stayed with his mother for four months. He would have gotten the nutrition he needed from her rich milk.

His mother would have taught him how to be a smart Vervet monkey. She would have cared for him for a year, while he learned to hunt. Then his mother would have stopped looking out for him.

Monkey Mothers and Babies

A primate mother bonds with her infant right after it is born. The mother knows her baby's smell. She knows how it looks and how it sounds.

Monkey babies are helpless when they are born. They would die if their mothers didn't care for them so well. The mother's instinct is very strong. If a mother loses her newborn, she may even adopt another mother's baby.

A mother monkey even kisses her baby. She will gently touch her mouth to her little monkey's lips.

Hundreds of other female monkeys would have cuddled him. They would have cared for him, a lot like his mother had done.

In Africa, Bob would have been busy. He would have played, hunted, and groomed himself all day. He would have "talked" to other monkeys. He would never have been lonely. He would have had many friends around.

Bob's new foster mom knew all that. She worried about Bob.

"She was aware of the problem, so she reached out to us," Eileen said. "She wanted to give him the best life possible." So, Bob's foster mom made a decision. The best life outside of Africa would be at the Primate Rescue Center.

CALEB

Like Bob, Caleb was a lively Vervet monkey. Only when he left the breeder who had raised him, he had no trouble finding a home. A man bought him. He kept Caleb in a cage when they weren't playing together.

Then Caleb's owner took a new job. He had to travel a lot. So, he hired a kind babysitter for Caleb.

Again and again, she took Caleb to her house when his owner was away. Soon she grew impatient. She would care for Caleb for weeks at a time. Then she would pack Caleb up and take him back home.

Bouncing from home to home was making Caleb afraid and shy. His babysitter worried. She asked Caleb's owner to let him live with her forever. He agreed.

The babysitter called the Kentucky Department of Fish and Wildlife. She wanted tips on keeping a Vervet monkey baby happy and healthy.

Instead, she found out that keeping Caleb was against the law in her town. Soon Caleb too was on his way to the Primate Rescue Center.

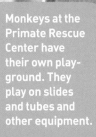

Monkeys at the Primate Rescue Center have their own playground. They play on slides and tubes and other equipment.

The Healing BEGINS

Suzie, Bob, and Caleb had found their way to safety. But they had not yet found each other. Caretakers at the rescue center had to get to know the monkeys first. Then they could help them feel truly at home.

It isn't good for a monkey to leave its mother too early. It makes it hard for the monkey to trust people or even other monkeys.

Suzie, Bob, and Caleb had all been taken from their mothers too soon. They would need time and help to heal.

At the Primate Rescue Center, the staff works hard to make the transition as easy as possible. "All primates are scared of strangers. Sometimes they seem mean. Suzie, Bob, and Caleb were shy and scared, but not mean," Eileen said.

Suzie, Bob, and Caleb each had their own cage at first. They were in a special building away from other primates. This is where they would spend their first few weeks at the rescue center. The building was calm and quiet. It was also filled with natural light. This helped comfort them a little.

It was the first sunlight Suzie had seen

for years. It helped her relax a little right away. The warm and quiet cage was just right, too.

The veterinarian at the rescue center gave each monkey a checkup. She put them to sleep, just for a little while. Then she looked each monkey over.

The vet took careful measurements of each monkey. She wanted to know how much they weighed and how long they were. This information helps the vet to help the monkeys.

If a monkey gains weight, it usually means it is happy. The monkey is doing well in its new home. If a monkey loses weight, the monkey may not be happy. Then the caretakers know the monkey may need more toys or more time with its caretakers. They watch closely to make sure each monkey is comfortable at the Primate Rescue Center.

The vet also took some blood from each monkey to test for diseases. Some diseases are caused by germs. Germs can hop from one animal or person to another. One blood test showed if the animal has disease germs. Other tests showed diseases not caused by germs.

It turned out Suzie had diabetes (sounds like die-uh-BEE-tees). Diabetes is not caused by germs.

If you have diabetes, your body can't use sugar in the right way. You are often thirsty. You don't have much energy. And you have to go to the bathroom more than an animal without diabetes.

Primate Toys

What kind of presents would keep a monkey happy?

Toys. Monkeys in zoos or rescues need fun toys to keep them active. You might think finding toys for monkeys would be hard, but the Internet makes it easy. Websites sell balls, blankets, swings, and tubes.

Primate toys are extra tough. They come in different sizes for different kinds of monkeys. Best of all, sometimes they come in different flavors. There are even monkey toys that taste like bacon.

Suzie couldn't spread her diabetes to other animals. But it made her feel terrible. She got diabetes from eating unhealthy food all her life. She would need a calm place to live. She would need a special diet and lots of water. She would need to take medicine for the rest of her life.

"Suzie was also very weak. She had not had room to exercise," Eileen said. "But she was so calm and nice. We knew she would adjust. She even took her medicine without a fuss."

Even better, Suzie loved her new meal plan. She ate lots of vegetables. She was on her way to a fit, new life.

Bob and Caleb weren't old enough to have such serious problems. They were each less than a year old when they were rescued. So, they got used to their new home faster than Suzie did.

"We gave them blankets and stuffed animals, so they had something to cling to," Eileen said. "That's a natural behavior for a young primate."

Bob got a healthy report right away. Little Caleb did not.

Caleb had a disease called worms. He had to take a special medicine to make the worms go away. The Rescue caregivers had to be very careful working with him. Otherwise, they could catch worms, too. Being sick helped Caleb because he got lots of one-on-one attention. It was just what he needed. Caleb began to feel better.

"All three of the monkeys were able to bond with the staff," said Eileen. "Soon they came out of their shells. They started to show their true personalities."

Suzie was shy, but kind and gentle. She loved to spend time with the Rescue caretakers. She loved to groom them. She would take her small monkey fingers and comb through the caretakers' hair to search for insects. If she found one, she'd remove it. She also loved to take bits of food from their hands.

Caleb was sweet, but shy and unsure. He would cling to his stuffed animals and soft blankets. He cuddled with them, rocking back and forth, back and forth. It was a sign he missed his mother.

Even so, he loved to play, once he got a little braver.

Bob was a lively, active little monkey. He had so much energy that he drove some of the other monkeys crazy. Bob would climb on them. He would wrestle them. He would nip and chatter and nudge them. He was trying to get them to play.

The monkeys were now getting the medical care they needed. They were getting to know their human caregivers. They were settling into the Primate Rescue Center. But something was missing.

It was time for each of the rescued monkeys to make friends.

Suzie the Olive baboon watches over Bob and Caleb. In the wild, female troop leaders would look out for young monkeys.

Chapter 3

A NEW Kind of FAMILY

Suzie, Bob, and Caleb didn't know it yet. But it was time for them to become friends with other monkeys.

"Some primates are introduced to a group or another monkey and everyone gets along fine," said Eileen. Finding those monkeys a rescue family is easy.

With others, it doesn't go so well. Making the right friendship match is a little harder with them.

Monkeys get along with their own kind in the wild. Monkeys raised by humans are different.

They haven't learned the things that help monkeys bond with each other. They haven't had to work together to find food. They haven't learned to groom each other. They haven't learned to trust each other. So, making friends can be hard.

Monkeys raised by humans are sometimes very scared when they meet other monkeys. They might act mean because they don't trust other animals yet.

The Primate Rescue Center keeps these monkeys separate from the other monkeys. They give them toys and activities. The toys, called enrichments, keep the monkeys happy and eager to learn. Often, they can see other monkeys in nearby cages. But they know those monkeys can't get too close.

The caretakers hope that these monkeys will calm down. They hope they will stop being so afraid. They hope they will someday be ready for friends.

It looked like Suzie might be one of those monkeys. The rescue center staff tried to put her with other Olive baboons. This made her afraid. She sat in the corner with her back to the other monkeys. When they came close, she screeched and ran away. She even bared her teeth to scare them away. She wanted nothing to do with them.

Leaving Suzie alone was the only choice, at first. The caretakers tried to make her happy in other ways.

Suzie had spent years of her life in a dark basement cage. This had made her pale and sick. The caretakers decided that Suzie needed fresh air and sunshine.

"When spring arrived, we moved Suzie's cage outside," Eileen said. "Right away, she seemed to bask in the sunshine. Her face tanned. She started to look like the Olive baboon she was meant to be."

Things were starting to get better for Suzie. One day they hoped Suzie could have a friend.

Bob's situation was different. He wasn't afraid of any monkey at the center. For a time, Bob was housed with Mighty. She was a macaque (sounds like mah-KAK) monkey who had come from a rescue center on Long Island, New York.

Like Suzie, Mighty had diabetes and needed a friend. But Bob had so much energy. He drove Mighty a little bit crazy. Bob and Mighty were not a good match.

Next, the caregivers decided to try pairing Bob with Suzie. And guess what? They liked each other!

Bob was smaller than the other Olive baboons, so Suzie wasn't so afraid of him. She was quiet, and Bob seemed to understand that.

Bob was still a crazy little monkey.

How Kids Can Help: Send a Care Package

Like other rescue groups, the Primate Rescue Center accepts cash donations to care for the animals. The center also has a wish list of items it hopes will be donated. If you see something you'd like to send, you can ship it to:

Primate Rescue Center
2515 Bethel Road
Nicholasville, KY 40356

Here are items from their wish list:

- ✓ Shredded wheat cereal
- ✓ Raisins
- ✓ Trail mix
- ✓ Nuts in shells
- ✓ Peanut butter
- ✓ Honey
- ✓ Graham crackers
- ✓ Pretzels
- ✓ Unsweetened coconut flakes
- ✓ Wood chips (pine, not cedar)
- ✓ Heavy brown paper leaf/yard bags

He buzzed around Suzie like a tornado. But she seemed to like watching him. It was odd, but the match worked. Suzie had a friend. And Bob had a quiet new granny.

Since Bob and Caleb were both Vervet monkeys, they seemed like a good match, too. So, the caretakers brought Caleb to the cage with Bob and Suzie. Caleb was a little shy at first. But in no time, Caleb and Bob were wrestling like brothers.

"You can tell Caleb looks up to Bob," Eileen said. "Caleb watches Bob and tries to be like him."

When Bob jumps into the sandbox full of sawdust to find hidden toys and treats, Caleb watches closely. He studies his brave new friend. Soon, he is ready to try the sandbox, too. When Bob swings or jumps or scampers, Caleb is usually close behind.

All three monkeys are close, Eileen said. "Usually, when primates are not closely bonded, they will walk away when another one comes near them. Or they will turn their backs and ignore them. That does not happen in this group. Suzie will sit by and watch the boys. They run by her and wrestle around her."

So, Suzie, Bob, and Caleb became a happy family. They live together and enjoy each other's company. They have plenty of food to eat. They have good care and exercise. Most of all, they have each other.

THE END

INDEX

MORE INFORMATION

To find more information about the animal species featured in this book, check out these books and websites:

Bats
Elizabeth Carney
National Geographic, 2010

Monkeys and Other Primates
Rebecca Sjonger and Bobbie Kalman
Crabtree Publishing, 2006

Tigers
Laura Marsh
National Geographic, 2012

Bat World
www.batworld.org

Carolina Tiger Rescue
www.carolinatigerrescue.org

National Geographic "Animals: Siberian Tiger"
animals.nationalgeographic.com/animals/mammals/siberian-tiger

National Geographic Kids "Animals: Creature Features—Tigers"kids.nationalgeographic.com/kids/animals/creaturefeature/tiger

National Geographic Kids "Amazing Bats of Bracken Cave"
kids.nationalgeographic.com/kids/stories/animalsnature/bat-cave

Primate Rescue Center
www.primaterescue.org

**To my father, who taught me to lead a compassionate life.
Love you, Dad. Always. —K.M.H.**

CREDITS

Inside This Book title page (in order of books, top to bottom): courtesy of Amanda Lollar/Bat World Sanctuary; Nicole Bregler/Primate Rescue Center; © IFAW/WTI S. Kadur; Title page, courtesy of Carolina Tiger Rescue; 4-5, Courtesy of Carolina Tiger Rescue; 6, Courtesy of Thomas County Sheriff's Office, Colby, Kansas; 13, Eric Isselée/Shutterstock; 16, Courtesy of Carolina Tiger Rescue; 23, Wild Bill Melton/Corbis; 26, courtesy of Carolina Tiger Rescue; 35, Jamie Grill/Photographer's Choice RF/Getty Images; 36, Courtesy of Amanda Lollar/Bat World Sanctuary; 38, Courtesy of Amanda Lollar/Bat World Sanctuary; 43, Jay Brousseau/The Image Bank/Getty Images; 48, Courtesy of Amanda Lollar/Bat World Sanctuary; 55, Joel Sartore/National Geographic Creative/Getty Images; 58, Courtesy of Amanda Lollar/Bat World Sanctuary; 67, James H. Robinson/Photo Researchers RM/Getty Images; 68-69, Nicole Bregler/Primate Rescue Center; 70, Nicole Bregler/Primate Rescue Center; 78, Nigel Pavitt/AWL Images RM/Getty Images; 82, Nicole Bregler/Primate Rescue Center; 87, Nicole Bregler/Primate Rescue Center; 92, Nicole Bregler/Primate Rescue Center; 98, SeDmi/Shutterstock; 102, Courtesy of Carolina Tiger Rescue

ACKNOWLEDGMENTS

Without the generous experts at the Carolina Tiger Rescue, Bat World Sanctuary, and the Primate Rescue Center, telling these stories would have been impossible. Thank you to these organizations and to all who are responsible for exotic animal rescues, for saving lives every day.

Runa and Kata
nuzzle each other.
They are as soft
and cuddly as
pet kittens.

Chapter 1

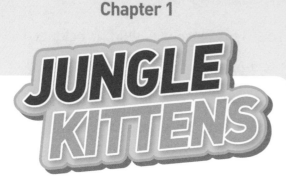

March 2009, Assam, India

People watched their step in the Assam (sounds like ah-SAHM) jungle in northeast India. Roads were few and made of dirt. Trees grew so close together they almost touched. And bushy plants and fallen logs covered the forest floor. You never knew when a hungry tiger or slithering python might surprise you. This place was wild. It belonged to the animals.

Two of those animals lay sleeping in a hollow tree. They were newborn kittens, or cubs. Their mother had left them alone while she went hunting for food. The cubs should have been safe. Except before the mama returned, some woodcutters came.

The woodcutters lived in a village on the edge of the forest, in a part of India called Kokrajhar (sounds like co-kruh-JAR). They earned money by gathering firewood to sell. One man saw the hollow tree. He chopped it down with his ax. The tree landed with a thud. Then he got a big surprise.

Two tiny furballs bounced out! The startled woodcutter dropped his ax. He scooped up the tiny cats. They mewed softly. Their gray spotted coats felt as soft as a baby chick. *What are they?* the man wondered. *Baby tigers or baby leopards?*

It didn't matter. The cubs were adorable. And there was no danger in picking them up. The babies' eyes hadn't even opened yet. *If only I could sell these cats*, he thought.

The woodcutter was very poor. He knew that wild-animal dealers would pay big money for the cubs. Then the dealers would sell the cubs for even more money. Rich collectors from other countries paid thousands of dollars for wild animals to put in their backyard zoos.

Even if no dealers came along, the cubs were a good find. Maybe the woodcutter could sell them as pets. Or his neighbors might buy them. Some men tied animal parts to their swords. This was a custom, or tradition, in his village. Some people hung animal skins up to decorate their huts. Local healers also used animal parts to make medicine.

The woodcutter knew it was wrong to capture wild animals. It was wrong to sell them too. The Indian government had laws against these things. But the thought of all the money he could make dazzled him. What if he could make $200 selling the cubs? That would be like winning the lottery! With that much money he could feed his family for many months.

The woodcutter carried the cubs home. Then he quietly spread the word. He had jungle cats for sale.

But his plan went wrong. He didn't know how to take care of the cubs. He didn't know how to feed them. Or even what to feed them! Another villager became worried. He told a forest department worker named Akhim (sounds like ah-KEEM) about the cubs. Akhim went to the woodcutter. He demanded the kittens. The woodcutter turned them over.

Akhim rushed the baby cats to the local wildlife rescue center. It was run by the Wildlife Trust of India. It was not a moment too soon. The cubs hadn't eaten in days. "One of them was seriously sick," says Sonali Ghosh (sounds like so-NAH-lee GOUSH). Sonali is an officer with the Indian Forest Service. "I was scared it might die," she said.

The rescue center veterinarians (sounds like vet-er-ih-NARE-ee-ens) examined the baby cats. "These are common leopards," the vets decided. The common leopard is the kind most "commonly" seen. There are also snow leopards, clouded leopards, and Sunda clouded leopards.

Everyone at the rescue center treated the cubs with great care. Workers fed the kittens around the clock. They gave them goat's milk, using baby bottles.

Leopards are meat-eaters. So the vets wanted the cubs to get a taste for meat. After about three weeks, the workers started mixing liver soup in with the goat's milk.

The cubs ate a lot. They grew fast. As they got bigger, the markings on their coats became easier to see. One day the vets noticed something very interesting. The spots on these cubs looked different from the spots on common leopards. They were darker and grayer.

The vets looked at each other. They wondered . . .

Could it be?

Yes! These cubs weren't common leopards after all. They were clouded leopards. Extremely rare, almost never seen, clouded leopards!

Which Is Which?

Clouded leopards and common leopards are both big cats. But they are not the same kind, or species (sounds like SPEE-sheez), of cat. They are as different from each other as lions are from tigers.

COMMON LEOPARDS

- Live in forests, plains, deserts, and mountains in parts of Africa, Central Asia, India, and China.
- Roar loudly.
- Weigh up to 106 pounds (48 kg).
- Are covered with small, dark-colored, round spots.
- Have feet that always face front.

COMMON LEOPARD

CLOUDED LEOPARD

CLOUDED LEOPARDS

- Live in tropical forests in Southeast Asia and India.
- Purr and meow.
- Weigh up to 50 pounds (22.7 kg).
- Are covered with large spots that look like brown and gray clouds.
- Can turn their hind feet so they face backward.

The higher the better for clouded leopard cubs! They play, eat, and rest up in the treetops.

A BOLD PLAN

Clouded leopards are very shy. They spend a lot of their time high up in trees. They are rarely seen in the wild.

The fact that these rescued cubs were clouded leopards changed everything. If they had been common leopards, the vets would have had to send them to a zoo. It's the law in India. That's because hand-raised common leopards lose their fear of humans. They might attack people if they were set free.

But clouded leopards don't bother humans. They hang out in treetops. Releasing hand-raised clouded leopards back into the wild would be OK. It would not put humans at risk.

But could these animals make it without their mother? Could they learn to protect themselves? Could they find their own food?

Bhaskar Choudhury (sounds like bas-CAR CHOW-durry) thought they could. So did Ian Robinson. Bhaskar is a veterinarian with the Wildlife Trust of India (WTI). Ian is the animal rescue director at the International Fund for Animal Welfare (IFAW). There was only one problem. IFAW had successfully released hand-raised elephants, bears, and even a tiger. But not a clouded leopard. No one had ever tried doing that.

The animal experts at WTI talked to the people at IFAW. They discussed what needed to be done. They talked about what could go wrong. Guess what? They decided to go for it! Everyone was super-excited to help save these rare animals.

Bhaskar and another vet, Panjit Basumatary (sounds like pan-JEET bo-SOM-uh-terry), went right to work. They put up a large cage out in the yard. They put blankets inside the cage for the cubs to sleep on. They also put branches inside it for the cubs to climb on.

Both of the cubs were males. The vets named one of them Runa (sounds like

RU-nuh). They called the other cub Kata (sounds like co-TAH).

The cubs had a lot to learn. After a few weeks, the vets started feeding them small chunks of cooked meat. Ian liked the cubs' reaction. "They would grab a piece of food and climb up in the branches to eat it," he says. "Climbing was instinctive [sounds like in-STINK-tiv] for them." In other words, they were born climbers.

The next step was getting them to eat their meat raw. That's what leopards do in the wild. So the vets began tossing dead chickens into the cubs' cage. Soon the cubs were eating plenty of raw meat.

In September 2009, Runa and Kata turned seven months old. They were big and healthy. They were eating well. It was time for them to learn clouded leopard ways. It was time to move them back to the jungle. But would the experiment work? Nobody knew.

Three men from Kokrajhar served as the cubs' keepers in the forest. They lived in huts they built themselves. The huts

were high above the ground. Each one was fitted between four trees. The huts had a bamboo floor, roof, and walls.

It was not easy work. Countless insects buzzed and whined all day and all night. They flew into the men's eyes and bit their skin. Cobras and other deadly snakes hid under bushes.

Mystery Cat

Clouded leopards are so seldom seen that scientists know very little about them. Here's what they do know:

1. Clouded leopards have very long tails, which help them balance on tree branches.
2. They use their hind feet to hang upside down from tree branches.
3. They eat birds, monkeys, pigs, small deer, and porcupines.
4. They ambush prey by leaping onto their backs and biting their necks.
5. They are good swimmers.
6. They are called "mint leopards" in China and "tree tigers" in Malaysia.

The keepers also faced danger from prowling tigers and charging elephants. That's why they put their huts up high—to stay out of the animals' reach.

For nine long months, the keepers lived like this. "These men were dedicated to these cubs," says Ian. "And brave. This was a tough job."

The keepers took turns, so that two men were on duty at the same time. The third would have the week off to return to the village for food and supplies.

Want to know what happens next? Be sure to check out the *Animal Friendship! Collection*

CREDITS